How to

Walk

Across America

And Not Be an A**hole

Vol. I

by
Tyler Coulson

The Walkout Syndicate

Chicago

The Walkout Syndicate LLC
Chicago, Illinois

thewalkoutsyndicate@gmail.com

Cover design by Everett Craven

ISBN 978-0-9856119-3-4

LEFT
RIGHT
LEFT
RIGHT
LEFT
RIGHT

BREATHE
EAT
SLEEP
BREATHE
SLEEP
EAT
BREATHE

I. INTRODUCTION

So you want to go for a long hike? Maybe the Appalachian Trail? The Pacific Crest Trail, or the Continental Divide? Or do you want to **walk across America**? I walked across America in 2011, so I know a thing or two about it.

This book is for professionals who are thinking of walking out (and who should probably take themselves less seriously) and for people who are insane enough to consider actually walking across the country. I fell into both categories before I walked out, and I could have benefitted from some clear, plain advice. I wish now that someone had shared the information in this book with me while I was hatching my plan, while I was planning the trip, or even while I was walking.

This is a practical guide to the knowledge and experience I acquired during my 2011 walk across North America. It is the result of answering emails and inquiries from interested folks. People contact me because they are planning a long hike or because they read my book, *By Men or By the Earth,* and want more information. I want to point people toward a sort of 'How To Walk Across America and Live to Tell About It' book, but there hasn't been one written.

I looked for a book like this before I walked across America. I found thousands of books about hiking and camping. Most are sprinkled with decent information surrounded by tons of garbage and marketing. Marketing! We're a generation of marketing consultants. This book is different: By the time you're done with it, you might feel that I'm the only person in the world who will never lie to you. You'll probably be right about that.

* * *

So I wrote this awesome book. Ideally, this book will help people who are planning long hikes. Hopefully, this book will empower

1

people to ignore bullshit. From time to time, stuff that I write in this book might also be bullshit. But maybe you'll be empowered enough to recognize those passages and to ignore them.

This book is not intended to catalog everything that one should know before attempting a cross-county hike—that wouldn't be possible in a single book, anyway. If you have any doubt about the intent of this book, please re-read the disclaimer at the beginning.

Walking across a continent is inherently dangerous. **You cannot rely on the information in this book as anything other than a primer to help you learn what to learn**.

I repeat, one more time, for legal *and* ethical reasons: **A cross-country walk is inherently dangerous. No representation is made that information contained in this book will work in your case. The author and publisher expressly disclaim any and all warranties, including but not limited to warranty of fitness for particular use.**

Get it? Your decisions are *your own*.

* * *

Let's get a couple of things out of the way.
1. This book is about thru-hiking. When I use the term thru-hike, I mean a cross-country hike that is completed within a single calendar year.
2. In this book, I refer often to the "Walker". The Walker is a construct, a mythical person who has decided to chuck it all and walk from coast to coast following *best practices*. It's important to remember that the Walker is a lot like Santa Claus, democracy, or healthy polygamous marriages—fun in theory, but they don't exist.
3. References in this book to "M.W.C" rules refer to the Model Walking Code. This edition includes the Model Walking Code as an appendix. I've developed the M.W.C.

to help people navigate life and walking. The M.W.C. is sometimes internally inconsistent, but that's life.

This book empowers you to not waste time on a bunch of crap, is really what it does.

This is going to be great!

* * *

M.W.C. 11: THERE ARE EXCEPTIONS TO EVERY RULE, INCLUDING THIS ONE.

There is no "right way" to walk across America. Every long hike is different and every long distance hiker is different. If you ask two long distance hikers the same question about routing or tents or footwear, then you are likely to get four or five different answers. I can offer only suggestions based on my experience.

Because there is no single right way, I enlisted three folks to help with this book. Nate Damm walked across the United States in 2011. John and Kait Seyal walked across the United States in 2012 with three therapy dogs in tow. These contributors do not agree with everything I have to say and I don't agree with everything they have to say, so I've marked all or most of their contributions with the name of the contributor. If it's not marked "—Nate Damm", or "—John Seyal" or "—Kait Whistler Seyal", then don't assume they agree with it.

* * *

Long distance hiking is physically and emotionally demanding, and one should consult a physician and a mental health professional before beginning anything like this. The highest priority should be coming home safely to family, spouse, children, pets, and friends, so do not try anything like this if you are not physically or emotionally capable of it.

But let's not kid ourselves. You're considering it, so you're almost certainly out of your mind already.

Let's get started!

A. Two Rules

M.W.C. 5: KNOW YOUR TRAIL, KNOW YOURSELF.

There are two hard and fast rules for the Walker: Know your trail, and know yourself. The rest are suggestions. If you go into a long-distance hike without knowing something of what to expect both from the trail and from yourself, then you will have a bad time—you may end up injured, dead, or crazy.

A(1) Know Your Trail

There are several established long-distance hikes in America and there are books and movies about these trails and how to hike them. The most popular trail is the Appalachian Trail ("AT") and second is probably the Pacific Crest Trail ("PCT"). Even some of the lesser-known but established trails, like the Continental Divide, East Coast Greenway, or Arizona Trail have trail resources available. But there are almost zero resources available for the aspiring transcontinental hiker—and with good reason. Walking across the United States is a dangerous endeavor and it is not to be taken lightly. Any sad sod can hike the AT or the PCT with a little planning. Those trails are like spoon-fed adventure.

"Oh, you hiked the AT? That must have been exciting and revelatory for you." But it wasn't exactly as challenging as a 3200-mile hike across an entire continent, across lowlands, prairies, grasslands, high plains, over the rocky mountains, across deserts, and more mountain ranges than you can shake a stick at…was it?

No. It wasn't.

* * *

Coast to coast is serious business, Folks.

If this book were a map made in the 1700s, the cross-country hike would be labeled "Turn Back Now! Here There Bee Monsters". The AT and the PCT are fun and relatively safe, with support networks in place and any number of resources to help you plan. You can challenge your body and your mind on an established trail, get away from the hum of modernity, and commune with thine own heart. You'll love it.

And it'll be a helluva lot safer than walking coast-to-coast.

But across the U.S.? Coast to coast? Alongside highways? Without designated campsites? You must be out of your mind! Know that, unless you are wealthy, you will be living like a bum. You will have many near death experiences. You will meet awful people, suffer awful weather, probably be injured, and will likely not make it all the way across. I do not know what the success rate is for a transcontinental hike, but I would estimate that probably eight out of ten people quit.

But I can't really talk you out of this, can I?

Of course I can't! Because you think that you'll meet wonderful people, have life-changing experiences, and will experience more joy than you thought existed in the world. You are correct.

For those few of us who are lucky and resilient enough to step into the other ocean after walking across a continent, life is never the same. We are not the same. We are happier, usually. More compassionate. Stronger. Faster. We have improved problem-solving skills, better stress-management skills, and better interpersonal skills.

We are better than we were.

* * *

A(1)(a) Finding a Long-Distance Trail

5

M.W.C 12.2: YOU CANNOT PLAN FOR EVERYTHING, BUT YOU CANNOT PLAN FOR *ANYTHING* UNLESS YOU KNOW YOUR TRAIL.

The first step is to decide which long-distance trail to walk. Many factors influence this decision and, again, there is no right answer.

Each established long-distance trail in the United States presents unique challenges. For example, the AT is physically demanding, but there are a lot of hikers out there, a well-established support network of people who have hiked the trail, and there is usually easy access to water. The PCT, by contrast, is longer, more remote, and has less access to water. On the AT you might see some black bears; on the PCT, you might see a grizzly bear. But both trails are rather internally consistent—meaning that you start in the mountains, you end in the mountains. More or less.

The American Discovery Trail is the premier coast-to-coast trail, running from Cape Henlopen, Delaware, to San Francisco, California. The ADT is an established network of trails, but it has nowhere near the type or level of support and access to resources that exist on the AT or PCT. It's bad form to expect the same number of "trail angels" on the ADT because walking coast-to-coast is so much more dangerous and difficult that few people do it. It's nothing like the AT or the PCT, and it's nothing like you expect it will be.

But you're going to do it, aren't you? Yes, I think you might.

* * *

One beauty of walking coast-to-coast instead of the AT or the PCT is in being free from established trails. It is probably best practice to stay on trail the whole time, but the westbound hiker discovers pretty quickly that there are no "trail police". There's no canon law on how to walk, where to walk, how to live. Out there you can go more or less wherever you want to go. There's no way to describe in words what that kind of freedom feels like.

Nate Damm is a certified member of Club 3200, a club that I founded. It's a small club; I sometimes pick new members who have walked across the country. Club members get a bumper sticker and a bunch of pride. I asked Nate what he thought about knowing your trail, and he said this:

> "Don't use the Goddamned American Discovery Trail for a thru-hike. Jumping on and off of it can be fun, but for a thru-hike it's needlessly long and inefficient."
> --Nate Damm.

I tend to agree. The American Discovery Trail is a great *local* resource for people who live near the ADT. It's great for weekend or day trips and is a great starting off point for planning a cross-country hike, but the negatives of staying on trail on the ADT probably outweigh the benefits on a thru-hike. The trail is not very well maintained in many places, the directions are often out-of-date, and in many cases the ADT actually directs hikers *away* from available resources. It's great…if you're on a bike.

* * *

No matter which trail you find yourself on, the Walker should know something of what to expect in terms of: 1) terrain, 2) weather, 3) access to food and water, and 4) potential dangers. I believe that a coast-to-coast hike along roadsides is by far the most dangerous long-distance hike in the United States, if not in the civilized world.

And it's also freaking awesome.

A(2) Know Yourself

The Walker should understand and respect his or her personal limitations. Too often, people discover their personal limitations at the worst possible time. On a Walk, this might happen on the first day, after a week, or after a month. It might happen fifteen miles from the nearest gas station or it might happen in the center of a city. It might be a physical problem, like collapsing from exhaustion, or it might be a mental problem, like losing your mind, stripping off all of your clothes, and running around slapping together the soles of your sandals to ward off evil spirits (or raccoons). The latter happened to me late one night in a campsite in Iowa. It was not a pretty sight, primarily due to the nudity.

The vast majority of people who consider a coast-to-coast hike never step up to the starting line. Of those who start, most won't make it all the way. Some will be injured, but most will simply quit; give up; go home. Many who quit will say they quit because "the hike just wasn't what I expected it would be". In most cases, that won't be true—most should say, "*I* just wasn't what I expected that *I* would be". There's no shame in not finishing a transcontinental hike, but there are a lot of easier, cheaper, and less dangerous ways to find out that you don't have what it takes rather than jumping into a trip like this.

M.W.C. 15: BE HONEST WITH YOURSELF.

* * *

M.W.C. 16: BE DAMNED HONEST WITH YOURSELF.

Anyone considering a long hike should recognize that it takes a great deal of effort and time to actually "know yourself". And no matter how well you think you know yourself, you will continue to learn every day on a Walk. The potential Walker should start listening to his or her body and to his or her *self*, or *soul*, or *mind* (or

8

whatever you want to call those thoughts and feelings inside the human head) *right now*.

The Walker must know how much food and water his or her body needs, when to eat and drink, how long he or she can go without a shower, how long he or she can go without a conversation with another person, how he or she will react if stranded in a violent storm, how he or she would react to a bear or a mountain lion in camp, etc., etc. This type of knowledge comes from having a highly developed working relationship with your own body and your own mind.

M.W.C. 17: YOU ARE THE BIGGEST VARIABLE IN YOUR OWN LIFE; DO WHAT YOU CAN TO PLAN ON THAT, IF NOTHING ELSE.

WHY?

WHY?

WHY WHY WHY?

WHY?

WHY!!!!!!

WHY!? !? !

BECAUSE I CAN.

II. The Why of the Thing

Best practice for a Walker is to examine his or her motivations for setting out on such a long trek. Why? There doesn't have to be a great answer—sometimes things just are what they are and there is no "why of the thing". But the Walker should consider the question for two reasons:

1. Thinking about the question provides personal insight into the Walker's motivations; and
2. The most common question a Walker hears is, "Why are you doing this?" Walkers should be prepared with an answer for that question.

* * *

Most cross-country hikers use the experience to raise money for or awareness of some cause. That's great. It's possible to raise both money and awareness by walking around with a sign, asking for donations, and doing workshops/visits along the way. John and Kait Seyal used their trip to campaign for therapy dogs, as an example, and they had great success with their blog, with media, and with therapy visits.

But a cause is not necessary.

Here are some reasons why a person might consider hiking across the U.S.:

- To see if he or she can.
- To test him or herself.
- To see the country.
- To meet people.
- To find one's "self".
- To raise money for a good cause.

- To raise money for a bad cause.
- To get in shape.
- To hide from an outstanding warrant.

Each of these reasons is noble in its own way. But none are required.

Western civilization brings us up thinking that everything has to be significant. But not everything has to be significant, not everything has to change the world, and not everything must have a *significant goal or destination*. A person can decide that this would be a meaningful, spiritual voyage of discovery…or just a good way to see the world without spending much money or leaving a very large carbon footprint. Whatever. If someone wants to raise money or awareness, great. But it's not required, and you shouldn't force an excuse-for-the-thing to masquerade as the why-of-the-thing.

M.W.C. 13: LIFE IS A PRACTICE; WALKING IS A PRACTICE.

* * *

It is best practice for a Walker to prepare a "Why of The Thing Answer" because every hiker gets that question over and over. Having an answer—even if it's not fully true—helps build trust between the hiker and strangers, it promotes legitimacy and compassion. So a Walk is more likely to succeed when the hiker prepares a Why of the Thing Answer to give to folks along the trail.

Do
You
Need
It?

III. Essentials

There are very few absolute essentials on a cross-country hike because there are so many variables and variations in experience that nothing can be guaranteed. Someone might be able to make it across the country without even a tent; some might not make it ten miles without a water filter. It's impossible to know everything.

There are, however, a few pieces of equipment that are so important that I believe the Walker *must* carry them. These are so important that I call them essential.

A. Essential Equipment

Cross-country hikers have to carry or push everything (unless they have car support, discussed in a different section) and so every ounce counts. Right now, you probably don't understand what that means in practice, but after a few weeks on the road cross-country hikers cut toothbrushes in half to save weight. Think about that. The Walker constantly considers each item's potential utility versus its actual weight, which is a difficult comparison to make.

All that uncertainty notwithstanding, the following items are a bare minimum essentials list:

- Water, including water purification tablets and/or filtration capability;
- Food;
- Shelter;
- First aid;
- Appropriate clothing, including many socks;
- At least 2 methods of starting a fire;
- Toilet paper or equivalent;
- Hiking stick, for protection and for ease in hiking;
- Knife;
- Tarp;

- Umbrella;
- Flashlight;
- Map.

This is the barest list of essentials possible and, depending on individual preferences and conditions, it might be incomplete. A hiker may want to take several other items and there may be several other things that a hiker needs at some point. But these are the barest essentials.

Let me be very clear: It is unlikely that a person would make it safely across the U.S. with *just* this list of essentials unless the person had a great deal of both luck and assistance from others. With luck, bare bones equipment like this list might get someone to safety, but even that wouldn't be certain.

B. Essential Planning

Here are the few things that I think the Walker *must* do before a long distance hike:

- Identify a general idea of the path to share with friends and family;
- Inform friends and family of the plan, but not expect them all to be supportive;
- Make all necessary arrangements for pet care, family matters, rent/mortgage, etc.;
- Arrange to stay connected with friends and family through phone, email, Twitter, Facebook, etc.;
- Designate a friend or family member as an emergency contact;
- Review equipment list *and* equipment.

Some of these suggestions may not apply to everyone, some may not be truly "essential", and again this list is not exhaustive. I planned my trip to a far greater degree, but almost all my plans beyond these few went out the window on the first or second day.

M.W.C. 20: Most "essential" planning is emergency preparedness; there will be emergencies.

If there's one thing for certain, it is that you cannot predict emergencies...but you can prepare for them.

B(1) When To Do It and In Which Direction

When to walk across America and in which direction are conjoined questions that must be considered together, like inseparable friends. Salt and pepper.

A hike that starts in the West is more likely to encounter bad weather. If a hiker starts in early spring in the West, then he or she will hit late winter weather in the Sierra Nevada and, potentially, the Rocky Mountains. That could mean death. Even if the hiker avoids death in the mountains, she'll be into the Great Plains during late tornado season, in the Midwest during the hottest and most humid part of the year, and then back into early winter territory in the East.

So most successful coast-to-coast hikes begin in the East at least by early March, if not mid- to late-February. It is a long way from the Atlantic to the Rocky Mountains, and the Walker must aim to get over the Rocky Mountains before the end of August. In fact, the Walker should probably be on the other side of the Rocky Mountains by the end of July if the Walker intends to cross the Sierra Nevada and finish in Northern California. If you need a reminder on why to fear and respect the Sierra Nevada, read *Ordeal by Hunger* about the Donner Party. Long story short: They got stuck up there in the snow and ate one another. Boom! Trip ruined.

The earlier the start, the better, more-or-less. This is because bad weather early in the year in the East is usually not so dangerous as bad weather in the Midwest or West. In the East, a Walker is never too far from a town or a house. And the people in the East are friendly enough that they often help in emergencies. There are some cold temperatures and rain in late February and early March, but there are also crystal clear, beautiful hiking days. If a hiker heads west at a good clip, it is unlikely that hot weather will hit until Indiana.

But, of course, there are no guarantees: I got hot weather the very first day I crossed into Ohio. C'est la vie.

M.W.C. 21: GO WEST; START EARLY.

C. Checklist

A physical checklist on a piece of paper is a great tool to help organize and memorize equipment before a long hike starts. A cross-country hike equipment list changes and evolves as the Walker learns more about the hike and more about him or herself. Managing a physical checklist can help commit the equipment inventory to memory.

With a physical checklist, it is also less likely that the Walker might leave behind something vital like the map. Yes, yes…I forgot my map. I had to postpone my first day of hiking for two days while my friend back home mailed me the map that I'd left on the kitchen table. You see, I was an idiot so that other Walkers won't have to be.

By halfway into the hike, the Walker won't need the checklist. The Walker knows exactly what he or she has and exactly where it is.

Breathe

IV. Equipment: Don't Get Hosed

Equipment is the first area in which people tend to get hosed. In my experience, the decision "I'm going to walk across the country" is followed quickly by the thought of "Oh, Man! I'm going to get a TON OF NEAT STUFF!". But slow down there, Speed Racer, because we're on a budget here. A Walk can easily blow a budget for two reasons: 1) You cannot plan for every contingency, and 2) Equipment is ridiculously expensive. It is best practice to save as much money on number 2 in order to have a few bucks in the sock in case of an emergency under number 1.

The weather blew my budget, for example. I was under most of the worst weather possible during my 2011 hike. I walked through unseasonable cold and rain in the East, then cold and rain and the Great Tornado Outbreak of 2011, then the hottest weather ever, including a "heat dome" in Iowa. As a result, I got stuck in motels way, way, way, WAY more than I intended. Nothing blows a cross-country budget faster than motels.

There will be emergency costs, if not because of weather then because of injuries, and if not because of injuries because of crime, and if not because of crime then because of emergencies at home, etc. Let's do our best to save money on the front end, Friend.

* * *

Long-distance hikers tend to be tech heads, so you are warned against striking up a conversation with a long-distance hiker about equipment unless you have a few hours to kill. They will go on and on about stoves and water filters, about tent materials and GPS systems. They will often mistake your inability to end the conversation with a willingness to listen; they will then mistake your "willingness to listen" for "sympathy with all of their own political beliefs". Soon they will talk to you about their "bug out bag", and what started as a conversation about preferred methods of purifying water turns into a long-from lecture on how FEMA is a front for the Illuminati and the New World Order. And ain't nobody got time for that.

Look: Get all that brand name and gear talk nonsense out of your head. I'm going to step through a consideration of quite a bit of gear and whether the expensive stuff is worth the extra cost. The good news is that quite a bit of the equipment people blow their paychecks on is either unnecessary or there are cheaper alternatives available.

M.W.C. 26: PACK LIGHT AND KNOW HOW TO USE WHAT YOU HAVE.

The Rules of Equipment boil down to these:

1) Have equipment that works,
2) That is as light as possible, and
3) Know how to use it.

If you don't know how to use it, then it's pointless to bring it along. And note that "is expensive" is not included in the Rules of Equipment.

A. To Carry or to Push?

The first equipment question for the Walker is whether to carry a backpack or to push some sort of a cart. This decision comes first because carrying capacity dictates what equipment will make it beyond the starting line. For example, if a hiker carries a backpack, then he or she likely cannot also bring a quarter panel off a 1972 Chevelle because there won't be room in the pack.

Most cross-country hikers begin their hikes carrying a backpack. They do it because it's rugged, idealistic. There is romance and beauty in laboring under the pack, carrying your home on your back, carrying everything you own in a knapsack. There is brutal honesty in doing the work and carrying the weight. Carrying a pack will make you strong and prove that you really accomplished something; it will build character.

Nonsense. The Walker should avoid carrying a backpack.

I started my hike with a backpack, as did many of the folks I know who attempted a cross-country hike. At least one of the cross-country dropouts I know of ended his hike in no small part because of the weight of his pack. If you are bound and determined to carry a backpack, I can't talk you out of it. But I'll try.

M.W.C. 11: PUSHING IS EASIER THAN CARRYING.

* * *

The trail often determines whether a hiker *can* use a pushcart or *must* use a pushcart. On the AT or the PCT, for example, conditions are comparatively constant and not quite as much equipment is needed. Moreover, the AT, the PCT, and similar treks are not conducive to using a cart because trails are often narrow.

But a cross-country hike involves a lot of roadside hiking. And trust me, backpacks get heavy very quickly. You think you're strong and tough, but if you hike 20 or 25 miles a day (I hit 40 some days on my trip), day in and day out for weeks, then you're not going to want to carry even 40 or 50 pounds on your back.

* * *

M.W.C. 3.1: YOU CANNOT CARRY ALL THE WATER YOU NEED IN THE DESERT.

In Utah, Nevada, and other parts of the arid West, there are very large distances without access to water—sometimes four or five days. That means that the Walker must carry all the water he or she will need until the next water source. A single hiker should count on drinking at least a gallon of water a day—in the heat, the Walker may drink three gallons of water per day. Water weighs about 8 pounds a gallon. (I'll give you a minute to do some math—that's 8 pounds per gallon x at least 3 gallons per day x 3 or 4 days between water + water for cleaning + emergency water). That's right—it's too much water to carry.

The Walker should get a cart.

Baby strollers designed for jogging are OK, but aren't very rough and/or tough. I used one from Iowa to Colorado and tore the crap out of it. Two other hikers I know made the same mistake—they got baby jogging strollers and tore the crap out of them. One hiker that I know of used a baby stroller all the way across, but it wasn't packed very heavy and it was a $500 unit, which is pretty expensive.

My cart of choice was a flat bed stroller designed to pull aged dogs behind a bicycle. It was made by a company called "Doggy Ride". I preferred it to the baby stroller for practical reasons, but also because a baby stroller attracts a lot of unwanted attention. Club 3200 member Nate Damm was stopped by the police about a hundred times in Kansas because motorists kept reporting a "Crazy dude with a baby out on the highway". No one wants that kind of attention.

A(1) Choosing a Cart

Here is what makes a good cross-country pushcart: 1) Collapsible, so it can fit into small spaces like car trunks, or through doorways; 2) large wheels, no less than 12 inches—but more than 20 inches is a waste; 3) enough space and weight limit to carry all, or most, of the equipment and a lot of water; and 4) brightly colored.

A cart needs to be collapsible because there will be situations in which the cart must be stowed in small places. There *will be* instances that require putting the cart in the back of a truck or a car's trunk. The cart must go through doorways, and some doorways are narrower than others. The Walker should learn to quickly collapse and re-assemble the cart.

Carts come with a weight limit that is a decent indicator of how much abuse the cart will take. Most jogging strollers are rated around 70 or 80 pounds. My first stroller, which I used from the Mississippi River to Denver, was rated around 80 pounds and I tore the ever-loving crap out of it with nowhere near 80 pounds on it. The frame bent, the tires were always flat, and the cradle that was designed to hold the baby ripped. I believe my Doggy Ride flat bed had a rating of around 120 pounds, and it was built like a tank. It was heavy and cumbersome, but I loved it because it never let me down.

Cross-country hikes require a lot of time spent beside highways, so the cart should be as brightly colored as possible to help bad motorists avoid hitting and killing the Walker. It's also a good idea to affix a tall flag to the cart, which makes the Walker and the cart much more visible to traffic.

The Walker needs a basic set of tools to fix the cart, too—but I mean basic. Carts are very simple, and the only necessary tools are likely a $1 tire changing kit, some spare tubes, and a wrench (which is sometimes included in the multi-tool that I advise hikers to carry).

M.W.C. 23.1: SOMETIMES A DOLLAR SPENT UP FRONT WILL SAVE TWO DOLLARS DOWN THE ROAD.

This Rule 23.1 is so important that I asked Nate Damm about it. He says:

> "Solid rubber tubes is a big deal for the cart. You should make a stronger push for them."
> –Nate Damm.

The Walker should swap out pneumatic tubes in the cart's tires with solid rubber tubes; they are more expensive, but they save a ton of time and money in the long run. Beginning in Iowa and continuing all the way through to the sea, pneumatic tubes are punctured again and again by nettles, thorns, and rusty nails. Each flat requires time to fix or repair, and there is a limit to how many times a tube can be repaired before it must be replaced. Solid rubber tubes are cost-efficient in the long run.

As for cost, the DoggyRide is a bit more expensive than the cheaper jogging strollers. That said, high-quality jogging strollers are expensive as hell. For example, I got a jogging stroller for about $100 and it was a piece of crap. The only stroller I know of that made it across the whole country retails for about $500. My DoggyRide Original Dog Stroller retails for about $250 and it could have made three more cross-country treks when I accidentally left it beside the road while changing a flat-tire on a rental car after I finished walking across America.

[*Editor's Note*: Neither the author nor the publisher have been in contact with the DoggyRide company and DoggyRide did not provide any financial support to the author's cross-country walk or for this book.]

Here's the recap for choosing a cart: collapsible, large wheels, enough space/weight, brightly colored, get solid tubes. Boom! Golden.

A(2) Choosing a Backpack

OK, so you're ignoring me on the cart thing? Got it. Well, you better pick the right backpack, then. Be careful: This is a place where people spend way too much money.

There are three types of backpacks: frameless, internal frame, and external frame. Frameless bags are simply bags with shoulder straps—think of Army duffel sacks. Frameless bags are versatile and wonderful in life, but are horrible for long-distance hiking, so I won't waste time discussing them. Internal frame backpacks are better in some ways, but are much more expensive. I carried an internal frame pack from Delaware to Iowa. However, if I had it to do over again, I would likely spend more time looking at external frame packs and I believe that the smart Walker would consider external frame packs.

A(2)(i) Capacity

Capacity is the most important consideration in choosing a pack. The large amount of equipment required for a cross-country hike necessitates a large pack. From the Atlantic to the Mississippi, the fact is that supplies are pretty easy to come by from day to day, so one could get by with a pretty small pack and just pick up food, water, etc., as he or she walks along. Still, it's better to always have three days' worth of food, water, etc., and to lug that huge pack on the back all day, every day. Talk about exercise and getting into shape!

Backpacks come in a range of sizes, from "day packs" at the small end with capacities around 20 liters, to the biggest packs ranging upwards of 80 liters. An 80-liter pack is about 4800 square inches, to give you another idea of size. Bigger, stronger hikers can carry bigger packs and heavier weights.

Along with capacity, *access* is an important consideration. The pack should offer quick, easy access to equipment, clothes, food, etc. I cannot begin to list all the possible configurations of pockets that mass market packs offer, so I won't even attempt it. Just go to a store or look online, and you'll find that some packs have smaller pockets on the sides or on the front of the pack. These are great features, because they allow the hiker to access frequently used items without rummaging through the main body of the pack.

The Walker will learn how best to use the pack, no matter what the configuration of pockets and zippers and straps.

* * *

M.W.C. 30.1: EXPENSIVE PURCHASES SHOULD HAVE MULTIPLE USES.

Any expensive purchase should have as many uses as possible. Packs are expensive—even cheaper external frame packs are usually more than $100. In the case of packs, one multiple use to look for is the ability to downsize the pack for smaller excursions.

Some internal frame packs have a detachable daypack on the top; that is a great feature. The Walker will pretty frequently find him or herself in camp, tent up, fire going, and then realize that he or she needs to hit up a store or a bathroom a half a mile away. A daypack makes it easier to accomplish little tasks like this without lugging around fifty pounds of gear.

A(2)(ii) Internal Frame or External Frame?

I am in the extreme minority here, in that I think external frame packs are a far better choice for a cross-country hike. Here's the big difference: An internal frame backpack has an aluminum frame that is sewn into the pack, so it looks very pretty, but the external frame backpack is a set of bags affixed to a big aluminum square-looking frame and wearing one makes the Walker look like an alpine adventurer. Internal frame backpacks are far more readily available. Most outfitters and hiking/camping stores carry a wide selection of internal frame packs.

Internal frame packs are nice when hiking through brush, because the internal frame is not exposed and will not snag on trees and brush. But, in my opinion, the advantages of the internal frame are outweighed by important design differences and by cost.

Internal frame packs carry weight with a lower center of gravity, so they are marginally safer and more stable to walk around in. This is a good design element if a hiker is crossing rougher terrain, climbing over downed trees, or navigating rough trails. But the trade-off is that the shape and structure limits their capacity to

24

comfortably carry heavy loads. Don't get me wrong, I used an internal frame pack and carried 100 pounds at the beginning of my trip—so it can be done. But it was very painful. The lower center of gravity of the internal packs causes the hiker to constantly lean forward when walking. That puts unnecessary strain on the back and hips.

External frame packs, on the other hand, carry weight much higher, so the hiker can walk standing straight up with the weight more evenly distributed between the shoulders and the hips. I guess if you are going to hike shorter distances over rougher terrain, an internal frame backpack is the way to go. But cross-country is a different ball game, Friend. Out there on the coast-to-coast, a hiker needs to get through long-mileage days on fairly easy terrain, and an external frame pack is fine for that job.

Due to marketing and market forces, external frame packs are about 1/3 the price of internal frame packs. That's a big difference, too.

M.W.C. 22: SAVE MONEY, ALWAYS.

* * *

Sometimes the best evidence for a particular method, product, or viewpoint, is that adherents to that view have very little to say. It's not always the case, but I think it is the case with regard to external frame packs.

I used an internal frame pack on my trip until I got a cart. I didn't hate every minute of it, but damn close. The Seyals both used internal frame packs until they got a cart, but they got a cart very early in their trip. (Note: I believe firmly that the Seyals got a cart so quickly because one among them, Kait, is a woman, and woman are 87.2% less likely than men to be complete and total idiots.) Consequently, we all have much to say about packs. Nate Damm, on the other hand, is the only one of us who escaped the internal frame pack mistake. What say you, Nate Damm?

> "I used a JanSport Carson external frame pack until I got a cart. Best pack ever and super cheap."
> --Nate Damm

That's the bottom line, right there.

* * *

When deciding what kind of pack to get, the Walker needs to know the trail and know him or herself. A majority of most cross-country hikes is on open trails/roadsides without a lot of brush, but with a relatively large equipment weight, so arguments in favor of an internal frame pack are not as strong. When you add in the fact that external frame packs are so much cheaper and look so much more bad-ass, it's really not a contest for me: External frame packs win the day.

A(2)(iii) Sizing

The Walker must make certain that the pack is the appropriate size and fits properly. There are generally three measurements that are important when sizing a pack: 1) the length of the spine, 2) the size of the shoulders, and 3) the waist size. All three dimensions are adjustable to one degree or another on most packs. Most packs allow the user to swap out hip belts for bigger belts (or belts that are more or less padded), and shoulders straps for bigger or smaller straps. Shoulder straps are usually adjustable on at least two points. The length of the pack *vis a vis* the spine is the least adjustable measurement and so is the most important factor in sizing a pack.

Because sizing is so important, best practice is to seek professional guidance while shopping for a pack. Any decent outfitter has a staff member trained in fitting a pack. Spine length will determine whether to start with small, medium, or large packs. (Or extra-large, for that matter.) Many packs can be fine-tuned in length—but this is usually an awful process, involving tearing apart bits of the pack that are fixed together tightly with Velcro to find the hidden mysteries of the pack frame. It's a huge hassle—so choosing the right frame length group is the important first step.

With the pack on, adjust the hip belt and shoulder straps to find a good fit. The hip belt buckle should ride just below the navel. On an internal frame pack, the shoulder straps should be in contact with the chest, shoulders, *and* back of the shoulders. The chest strap should not be so tight as to pull the shoulder straps close together.

Once a pack is identified that *might* fit, it needs a test-run. The wise shopper will fill the pack up with 30 or 40 pounds of weight and wear it around the store or on a short hike before purchasing it. Most stores have sandbags laying around for this purpose. Each pack will wear differently when it is packed and when it is empty, so it's vitally important to wear it while weighted.

* * *

Here's a lesson in why it's important to get a properly sized pack: During my first two weeks on the road, I was overcome every day with awful pains in my chest and in my left arm. I thought I was dying of a heart attack. I pulled over to the side of the road several times each day to take my pack off, lie down, and swallow aspirin. I was certain that I would die.

But here's the kicker: All of that pain in my chest and in my left arm was caused not by heart attacks, but by a pack that did not fit properly and wore too heavily on a nerve in my left shoulder. I got re-sized for a new pack about two weeks into my Walk. I replaced my pack with a longer framed model and the pains went away immediately.

* * *

M.W.C. 35.1: DON'T RELY ON EQUIPMENT UNTIL YOU'VE LEARNED HOW TO USE IT.

The Walker should wear his or her pack fully loaded on a few long hikes before heading out for a Walk. The pack is an expensive and important item, so the Walker should know it inside and out before relying on it.

B. Water

In this section, I'll discuss water and carrying capacity. This is a great place to trim costs. I put this section near the beginning of this book because water is *the most important thing in the world*.

M.W.C. 3: PLAN FOR WATER, ALWAYS.

* * *

When people think of long-distance hiking, they often think of stopping beside a clear running brook to gather water. That may very well be the case on many long treks—on the AT, for example, there are any number of creeks and springs that one can drink from if there has been a decent amount of rain that season. But this is not the case when walking across America.

A cross-country hike doesn't present constant (or even very good) access to surface water, whether river, creek, or lake. Accordingly, the Walker relies largely on municipal water supplies, which means that the Walker must carry enough water to meet his or her water needs until reaching the next water source. To do this, The Walker must understand:

1) Personal water needs;

2) Access to water; and

3) Carrying capacity.

Obviously, this greatly increases required carrying capacity.

Prior to beginning a cross-country hike, the cross-county hopeful should have a sense of personal sweat rate and how much water will be necessary to replace fluid levels. Hiking eight to fifteen hours in the hot, hot heat requires a lot of water. A good rule of thumb that I have heard is to drink plenty before you start hiking and then drink at least a pint of water an hour.

[*Editor's Note:* There is a lot of debate about how much people should drink while hiking. A pint per hour might be overkill and, for some, it might not be enough water.]

Now, a liter is a little over two pints and there are about eight pints in a gallon, so that is a *minimum* of two gallons in an eight-hour hiking day just for drinking. Now add to this amount the water you need to wash dishes after dinner and at least a pint to wash your feet (more on this later). It adds up, now, don't it?

When planning for water, the Walker should try to plan at least two days in advance, considering both needs and access. There is usually access to water in towns, but there is very rarely water out in the middle of nowhere. In emergencies, of course, the Walker is very rarely so far from a home that he or she couldn't collapse from dehydration on a stranger's front porch, point at his or her parched mouth, and mouth the word "water".

Now, as for carrying capacity, there are a million high-tech, expensive ways of carrying water around. I think they are mostly a waste of money. Some people disagree.

B(1) Water Bladders

Some people swear by the use of water bladders. I think they are a waste of time and money. A few companies—like Camelback and

Platypus—make water bladders that can be worn as a backpack or integrated into an existing pack. These have a siphon or straw that allows the wearer to drink on the move. While these are useful for ultra-marathon runners and for folks who are hiking for speed, they are not necessary for a long hike and, in my experience, usually cause more trouble than they are worth. These are certainly not *necessary* for a cross-country hike, but some people enjoy having them.

Let's be honest: Most of us are not famed Tour de France non-winner Lance Armstrong. We're not out to break any records and most of us are not super-soldiers designed by the government. We're just regular folks, so let's just step back and look at this rationally. Drinking vessels like, say, water bottles are technology that's been tested and proven for about 20,000 years. Water bottle technology works well and is a heck of a lot cheaper than Camelbacks and "hydration systems".

Of course, I've known cross-country folks who have used these types of systems with varying degrees of success. Kait Seyal, for example, swears by her Platypus hydration system. She says she's not particularly good at remembering to take breaks to drink water—and that is dangerous in the hot weather. But with the water bladder straw right there at her shoulder it wasn't a problem for her to remember to drink throughout the day.

B(2) Water Bottle

The Walker needs two functional water bottles. (Many hikers set off with several, strangely enough.) This is a good place to cut costs by not spending big money on super-expensive bottles made of "unbreakable" plastic. Both unbreakable plastic bottles and spun aluminum water bottles are heavy and expensive. Instead, there are bottles made of the softer white plastic like you used to see high school basketball teams drinking from. They are cheap and they work just like any other drinking vessel in recorded history. I carried one of these on my cross-country hike—I found mine at REI, although it looks like this type of bottle is no longer available at the REI website. They might still carry them in the stores, though; I haven't checked. I also carried a slightly nicer bottle, and I think it was a waste of money. The softer kind often come with hash marks on the side for measuring out ounces—that comes in handy for measuring water for cooking.

M.W.C. 30.2: RE-USE, REPURPOSE; THE DEAD AND DESIGNERS HAVE NO RIGHTS.

Many long distance hikers don't buy water bottles at all; instead, they re-use soda bottles or sports drink bottles. This is because long-distance hiking has the capacity to turn idiots into rational, thinking folks. So instead of buying expensive water bottles or hydration systems, the Walker might consider re-purposing soda bottles and sports drink bottles.

B(3) Carrying Capacity

In addition to a water bottle (or bladder) to drink from, the Walker needs the capacity to carry enough water in reserve for drinking. In the western deserts, I sometimes had to carry ten or twelve gallons at a time. That's upwards of 80 pounds of water. How to store this water? Easy: Re-use gallon water jugs.

Gallon water jugs or orange juice jugs make great reusable water reservoirs. But my preference is for the cylindrical gallon jugs that are stackable.

Water jugs with screw-on caps are far better than the type with click-on caps. The click-on caps always pop off and leak water all over your expensive blogging equipment.

B(4) Getting Water On the Road

When on-trail, a large portion of the Walker's water comes from garden spigots and park spigots. However, each cross-country hiker must at some point re-fill water bottles out of a faucet in a kitchen or a bathroom. This presents a challenge because most water bottles don't fit underneath standard bathroom faucets, and no gallon jugs fit under most faucets. I learned this the hard way.

The solution is to get a short length of hose and a camp fuel funnel, both available at most sporting goods stores, outfitters, or farm supply stores. The hose and funnel cost about $1.50, and are worth it. Connect the funnel to the hose, put the funnel under the faucet and the other end of the hose in the water jug, and boom! Golden.

* * *

A Walker will at some point have to fill water jugs from a friendly person's garden hose (or might resort to scrounging water from the garden hose of some unsuspecting household). Water sits for ages in those hoses, becomes stagnant, and hosts diseases. Unless you grew up like I did, drinking almost solely from a garden hose and sleeping in a hay barn, then you probably have no immunity built up to such pathogens and parasites. So it is best practice to let that hose run a while to flush out the stagnant water before filling up. You'll be glad that you did and you might not get dysentery and die.

B(4)(a) Water Purification

Something like 99% of the water on a cross-country hike comes from municipal sources. Still, it is possible that the Walker will at some point have to take water from a stream or river. In the olden days, you could do this freely and not worry about death because surface water was all safe and pure and wonderful. Now, not so much—most naturally occurring surface water on a cross-country hike are contaminated to one degree or another. So the Walker should have the ability to purify water in emergencies.

There are four primary methods of purifying water. They are: 1) boiling, 2) adding purifying agents, 3) ultraviolet light, and 4) filtering. Each has advantages and disadvantages.

* * *

I will discuss each of the purification methods mentioned above, but first the Walker should have an idea of what kind of contamination the water might harbor, what water should be avoided, and how to remove debris from the water.

There are three general types of contamination one can expect in surface water: biological, chemical, and what I call gunk. Biological contaminants are microscopic organisms like protozoa, bacteria, or viruses. Biological contamination can cause all sorts of gastrointestinal problems—think: *Montezuma's Revenge*. The second type of contamination is chemical, which usually results from run off from agricultural fields or mining operations. The third type is *gunk*, and that's all the dirt and particulate matter that, while it might not kill or sicken, certainly doesn't taste or smell good.

Identifying safe surface water is difficult. Some water may appear cloudy and not smell good but might be safe; the opposite might also be the case. There any number of resources on the Internet where one can read about how to identify safe (or safer) surface water, but a few tips are pretty much common sense:

- Running water is generally safer than stagnant water.
- Don't drink from pooled water that contains dead or decaying animal corpses.
- Avoid drinking from run off from cornfields or other agricultural areas.

- Avoid drinking water that is run off from mining operations.
- Avoid water that smells strongly of contaminants.
- Avoid standing water on or near highways.

Some hikers look for signs of insect life on or near the water to indicate safety. I'm sure that's a helpful indicator, but I doubt that it's 100% safe. Some hikers sniff the water and, if it smells good, they drink it—again, I don't think that's 100% safe.

The best practice is to take all reasonable steps to purify any surface water before drinking. These steps may involve filtering, treating with iodine, or even boiling. Some purification steps may be *overkill*, but it's always better to be safe than sorry.

* * *

Two pre-treatment steps that can make gathered water both safer and much more enjoyable to drink are cloth filtering and allowing sediment to settle. These steps *do not* remove dangerous contaminants and *do not* necessarily make water safe for drinking. They do, however, make water clearer (which is necessary if the water is to be purified with UV light), and tend to make the water more aesthetically pleasing to drink. These steps are not a substitute for purification processes and should be used in conjunction with chemical treatment, filtering, or boiling.

First, use a handkerchief over the opening in a water bottle to filter out large impurities in the water. This will remove some of the sediment, as well as little bits of rock and vegetative matter. Then allow the cloth-filtered water to sit still for a while; the heaviest sediment matter in the water will settle to the bottom. This might take an hour or more. The clearer water at the top can then be poured off into another water bottle.

Doing this will make the water taste and look better. It will greatly improve the effectiveness of a UV filter (discussed below) and will greatly prolong the life of a pump action filter (also discussed below).

* * *

Boiling is the traditional method of purifying water and is the most effective at eliminating biological contaminants, like giardia. At sea level, water boils at 212 degrees Fahrenheit, at which temperature most biological contaminants will die, leaving the water safe to drink. Water heated to sub-boiling temperatures for longer periods of time can also be made safe for drinking—this is the principal behind pasteurization. Some contaminants are more resilient than others and might require more time at a boil to destroy, but the famous parasites like giardia and cryptosporidium die when water is brought to a boil.

Boiling is not likely a winning strategy for the cross-country hiker, however, because it takes a lot of time and requires a lot of fuel. In some situations, boiling might be the best option, but it should not be the Walker's *only* emergency water purification strategy.

Moreover, it's important to remember that naturally occurring water is as likely to be contaminated with chemical agents from runoff, whether from agricultural operations in the Midwest, or mining operations in the East and West. It is, generally speaking, difficult to remove chemical contaminants like these from water and boiling will *concentrate* such contaminants. A little bit of these chemicals and metals might not kill a hiker, and might not cause the hiker to grow a fourth arm and flippers, but it certainly ain't the pinnacle of healthful living, either. Where these types of contaminants might be present in water, it's best to not rely on boiling.

35

* * *

Probably the most common (and cheapest) method of purifying water is adding a chemical agent. The two most common agents are iodine and bleach. Iodine is available in tablet form, usually marketed as "water purification tablets", or something similar. Bleach is…well, bleach. It's available all over the place.

These methods have drawbacks, of course. It takes time for the iodine or bleach to propagate through the water and kill biological contaminants, and the temperature of the water will impact how quickly the water will be safe to drink. Additionally, neither is 100% effective.

Those drawbacks notwithstanding, iodine tablets are probably the most useful, cheapest, lightweight, and easiest to use method of purifying water. Water treated with iodine will not taste good, and I've heard that prolonged use of water treated with iodine can lead to kidney damage and thyroid problems. I don't know if any of that is true, but short-term use of iodine-treated water in adults with a healthy thyroid probably shouldn't cause a problem. The Army uses iodine. Other crazy survivalist people swear by iodine treatment. And fifty million Elvis fans can't be wrong.

* * *

Ultraviolet light (like the kind of radiation that comes…*from…THE SUN!*) is a pretty sweet tool for sterilizing things. High falutin' medical doctors sometimes use it to sterilize medical equipment and surfaces. There are various UV-treatment tools available to sterilize water, as well.

UV filters are battery-powered lights that emit UV radiation. When submerged in water for the required period of time, the UV rays kill just about every living thing in the water, from bacteria to protozoa to very small Hollywood actors (like Joe Pesci, or Tom Cruise). They do not work well at all in cloudy, unfiltered water, because the particulate matter in the water blocks the UV radiation and the little would-be Oscar award-winning protozoa hide in the shade.

This method requires certain conditions that are unlikely on the trail, though, and so I do not favor it. While UV filtering is both sweet and awesome, it's not really a reliable method of filtering water on the trail.

* * *

The last method worth discussing is filtering. In my experience, this is the most likely to lead to good tasting, clear, safe drinking water. The drawbacks are substantial, though—weight, cost, and inconvenience.

Some pump action ceramic filters are claimed to remove all contaminants down to .2 microns in size. That's pretty small. Some viruses might slide through, like Hepatitis or what have you, although the modern ceramic filters often claim that most viruses will not pass through the filter. Some pump action filters also employ a carbon filter, like charcoal, which greatly improves the taste of filtered water.

I carried with me a Katadyn filter—and I only had to use it *twice*. At first blush, it seems like it wasn't worth the expense in dollars or extra weight. But the kicker there is that I had to use it twice. Think about that. It was nowhere near worth the money I paid for it or the weight of it, except that I had to use it twice and might have died without it. It made me feel safer, but I didn't really need one that nice, expensive, or heavy. On the AT or the PCT, it would have come in handy. But out there on the American highway, there simply isn't enough chance to use one to justify much expense. At any rate, there are far cheaper alternatives available now to purify small amounts of water at a time.

If a Walker chooses to rely on a filtration system for emergency water needs, he or she should look for a lightweight, backcountry filter. They can run as little as $60.

* * *

Note that whatever vessel is used to initially gather water will be contaminated with any biological agents present in the water. Treated or filtered water should never be put back into gathering vessels. Likewise, if using a pump action filter, the out spout must never come in contact with unfiltered water.

Once out of danger, all vessels should be cleaned with water that is known to be safe.

C. Tent and Shelter

The Walker must carry shelter. A tent is recommended even if the Walker has car support. It should be a high quality, lightweight, freestanding, three-season tent. The tent is one of few pieces of equipment that should *not* be brightly colored. This is one area where money can be saved, but it's justifiable to spend more money for a higher quality tent.

There are a number of different styles of tents/shelter available, of 3 basic types: 1) bivouac style, 2) tarp shelters, and 3) tents. A cross-country hike requires a shelter that is lightweight but large enough to accommodate a hiker, some basic equipment, and any hiking partners, as applicable. Privacy and comfort are important because a Walk isn't a 3-day weekend or even a 10-day backcountry outing, it is a temporary lifestyle.

A bivouac sack or bivy shelter is lightweight, but the savings in weight are offset by less comfort and convenience—a hiker in a bivy can't bring a pet, for example, or have any overnight visitors. We're all adults here—most hikers want overnight visitors from time to time. A bivy shelter does not provide enough comfort or privacy for a cross-country hike and it is not as adaptable as other shelters.

A truly hardcore hiker could consider a basic tarp shelter. Those who are so inclined can learn to make a typical triangle style or A-frame style shelter with just a pole, a tarp, some tent pegs and rope. The whole set up costs about $15. I love this style of tenting because it's cheap, adaptable, and super lightweight. However, if you're an office-type, you're probably not up to living underneath a tarp shelter. It provides less protection, less privacy, very little or no ground protection, and it takes a relatively long time to pitch a tarp shelter. Plus, many areas of the United States are absolutely crawling with bugs, creepy crawlies, chiggers, mosquitoes, and wee, sleekit, cow'rin, tim'rous beasties. On a coast-to-coast hike, the wise Walker skips the tarp plan.

In my opinion, a tent is necessary for a solo thru-hike. A single year, unassisted or largely unassisted thru-hike requires shelter that provides a substantial amount of protection at minimal weight and that is easy and quick to pitch and to strike in all environments. You can only get all of that with a lightweight tent.

Nate Damm agrees:

> "Don't be dumb; get a tent. The first morning that you wake up with bugs coated all over the outside of the tent you'll be damn glad you didn't spend the night under a tarp. Bugs suck. They are everywhere. Especially in the Midwest."
> --Nate Damm

For a cross-country hike, the way to go is a three-season, double-walled, freestanding tent.

Some tents are described as "summer tents", some as "three-season" tents, and some as "four-season" tents. Four-season tents are those amazing, awesome, tube shaped homes you see on Mt. Everest or at MacMurdo in Antarctica. They're great, but they are way too heavy and expensive. A three-season tent is the way to go.

"Double-walled" refers to the tent consisting of an outer "wall", which is a rain fly, and an inner "wall", which usually consists of little more than mosquito netting. Single-walled tents, by contrast, consist of a single, thicker layer of tent material. A double-walled tent will generally have better ventilation, better insulation, and will have fewer problems with condensation inside the tent. Moreover, in the hot, hot heat of the Summer, the rain fly can be left off, allowing the tent a great degree of ventilation and cooler sleeping.

M.W.C. 31: VERSATILITY IS POWERFUL.

The tent should be freestanding because a freestanding tent is a versatile tent. A freestanding tent, as the name implies, can be pitched without staking the tent out. That might not sound like a big deal, but the first time you try to pitch your tent on a concrete slab, you'll sleep all night long on the cold hard concrete in the rain and wishing that you'd listened to me.

* * *

The tent is home for a long-distance hiker for a long while, so the tent should be respected. A cross-country hike pushes the limits of any tent, and any added stress—whether a pet, or bad weather, or multiple campers—will shorten the life of the tent. Most hikers get across the country with just one tent, but it's in pretty bad shape by the end. I went through three tents when I walked across America.

Product Endorsement: The Big Agnes tent company makes amazing tents. I'm not going to lie: They are pricey. But these tents are absolutely killer products. The Big Agnes Fly Creek UL-2, for example, weighs about 2 pounds when fully packed with pegs and a rain fly, and it sleeps two somewhat snugly and one like a freaking hotel room. I used a Fly Creek UL-2 from West Virginia to Nevada until Mabel or I ripped it in the middle of the night. (I believe that John and Kait Seyal used a Big Agnes tent, as well, that lasted them from coast-to-coast.) I was so impressed with the product that I replaced it with another Big Agnes tent. The Big Agnes products might not fit in everyone's budgets, but, in my opinion, they are a great example of what to strive for in choosing an ultra-light tent.

[*Editor's Note:* Neither the author, the publisher, nor any contributor has talked with the Big Agnes company, and Big Agnes has not provided any money or sponsorship in connection with the author, the publisher, or this book. I will likely send them a copy of this, though, and say "Hey! Can you help a brother out!?"]

* * *

M.W.C. 38: WHEN YOU NEED TO HIDE, BE HIDDEN.

The tent is about the only item that should not be brightly colored. When choosing a tent, the right-minded would-be Walker looks for a muted green color. The Walker should struggle to be seen when walking along a highway, but it is sometimes necessary to be hidden when camping.

* * *

M.W.C. 22.4: DON'T LET ANYONE SELL YOU SOMETHING THAT YOU DON'T NEED.

Sporting goods stores, outfitters, and tent manufacturers try very hard to sell "footprints" for tents, but they are not necessary on a cross-country hike. A footprint is an extra piece of material, usually nylon and usually a bit heavier than the tent material. It goes on the ground underneath the tent and it protects the tent floor from puncture from rocks and pinecones and things.

Footprints are heavy, expensive, and almost always a waste of money for a cross-country hiker. I used a very, very lightweight tent and hardly ever put anything between it and the ground and never once had a puncture. That tent finally ripped in Nevada, but it ripped from over use *and*, when it finally ripped, I *did* have a tarp beneath it.

They are doubly unnecessary because, in the "selecting your campground" section, I explain that one should prepare the ground to accept a tent before pitching the tent.

Tent footprints are triply unnecessary because a tarp is an essential item and can double as a footprint in a pinch. A tarp is about a billion times cheaper than a footprint and is an essential item, so there is very little need to waste money and weight on a footprint.

C(1) Sleeping Bag and Accoutrement

A sleeping bag is not included in the essentials list, but only because the equipment on the essentials list is enough to get the Walker to a store to get a sleeping bag. There is cold weather at the beginning of a cross-country hike, again in the Rockies from time to time, and again during desert nights, so a sleeping bag is essential for a successful cross-country hike. Depending on the individual, a sleeping bag might even be necessary in the warm Midwest.

Sleeping bags run the range from very cheap to very, very expensive. Funny story: I got a sleeping bag for $3 at Target. I think it was mismarked, but that's how it rang up. I ended up sending that one away in favor of a lighter, higher quality bag, but that's neither here nor there. I still have that $3 bag and I still use it all the time. In fact, it's my main bedding at night when I sleep on the floor of my flophouse apartment. It keeps me warm and safe as I dream of a day when I'll have enough money to pay off my student loans *and* pay for health insurance. Yes, a good sleeping bag is important.

There are quite a few different types of sleeping bags. Most importantly, sleeping bags come with different temperature ratings. Additionally, there are bags insulated with down and bags insulted with synthetic materials. Then, there are generally three different shapes of sleeping bags—rectangular, mummy, and hybrid. Both the mummy-style and hybrid-style bags can come in shapes specifically designed for men and women.

* * *

The most important factor when choosing a sleeping bag is temperature rating. Temperature ratings reflect the lowest temperature at which the sleeping bag manufacturer thinks that you can sleep in the bag and not die of hypothermia. For example, if you have a sleeping bag rated to 35 degrees and you sleep out in 10-degree weather, then you are going to die.

Temperature ratings are only averages, and are notoriously unreliable. I've heard a general rule of thumb is to identify what is likely to be the lowest nighttime temperature for a given hike and then to get a sleeping bag rated for 20 degrees lower. So, using this formula, if the nighttime low is likely to hit 30 degrees Fahrenheit, then the Walker should get a bag rated to 10 degrees Fahrenheit. That sounds like a pretty decent rule of thumb to me.

A number of factors will increase or decrease the effective insulation of a sleeping bag. Extra layers of clothing add warmth, of course, and a properly pitched tent of the appropriate size adds about 10 degrees of protection because body heat warms the tent.

* * *

There are three general sleeping bag shapes. Rectangular bags are...drum roll...rectangular. Rectangular bags are my preference because I move a lot when I sleep and because it is easier to ventilate and let heat out of a rectangular bag than the other shapes. Rectangular bags allow me the room I like to have when I thrash around all night through a forest of nightmares. These tend to be the cheapest, as well. The very big downside of the rectangular style bag is that they are much, much heavier due to the extra material.

What I call "hybrid" bags, are really just tapered bags. They are shaped a bit like a cone—imagine a rectangular bag that tapers down to a narrow foot area. Some hybrid bags also flare at the shoulders. My current backpacking bag is a hybrid bag and it does the trick—it's a similar sleeping experience as a rectangular bag, but with much less weight.

The third type is the mummy-style bag. These are the bags that are relatively form fitting and have a hood at the top. These things zip up until only your face isn't covered. I hate these things.

Hiking and camping literature all indicates that mummy-style bags are the warmest. (Personally, I don't know if I buy that theory or not.) There is very little room to move around in these things, so they are not ideal for a person who sleeps violently.

For the cross-country hiker, a mummy-style bag is probably the best decision because they generally offer a greater degree of warmth at substantially less weight. But, like all good things in a world of good things, they tend to be the most expensive.

* * *

Shocker: Men and women are shaped differently.

Some sleeping bags are shaped for men and some are shaped for women. Sleeping bags should be chosen accordingly.

Beyond that, it's important to try a sleeping bag on and get the right fit. If the sleeping bag is way too large, it won't insulate as well. If it's so small that it fits tightly, then it won't insulate because the fill material will compress and squeeze the air out of it. As a general rule, I believe that a sleeping bag should be large enough to leave ample room for two or three extra layers of clothing and a bag liner, but not much larger.

* * *

Sleeping bag liners are lightweight bags/sheets that slip inside the sleeping bag, creating an extra layer. These are great and, budget permitting, can be a great help on a cross-country hike. Sleeping bag liners provide as much as 10 degrees of extra cold protection, and, *if you're like me*, then a sleeping bag liner is warm enough to sleep in many nights in the late Spring and Summer.

The unsung greatness of sleeping bag liners is that they protect the inside of the sleeping bag so that the bag will need cleaning much less frequently. Unlike sleeping bags, liners can readily be laundered. So that is a benefit.

* * *

Sleeping bags are filled with either down or synthetic materials. There are benefits and detriments to each, of course.

The general consensus seems to be that down sleeping bags are great and awesome and wonderful. They are also much more expensive.

Synthetic bags fare far better with moisture. A synthetic bag will still insulate a bit when it gets a little wet, but down won't insulate at all if it gets wet. A wet down sleeping bag weighs about 7000 pounds and is completely worthless as a sleeping bag.

Now, when dry, I'd say that a down sleeping bag is a bit warmer and a bit more comfortable than a synthetic bag. When dry, a down bag is usually lighter than a synthetic bag with a similar temperature rating. And down bags pack down a bit smaller than a synthetic bag. So they're great in all those ways.

But for my money, a synthetic bag is a better choice for a cross-country walk. I prefer the synthetic bag for a cross-country hike first because of the price difference, which is substantial, and second because it's nearly impossible to avoid wet conditions on a hike so long. Synthetic bags perform so much better under wet conditions (and dry so much more quickly) that I think they are a better product for a cross-country hike.

* * *

M.W.C. 48.1: DON'T SLEEP WET.

A good hiker does all that is possible to keep the sleeping bag dry. When packed, the bag should be stored in a waterproof container such as a dry stuff sack or a trash compactor bag. I prefer trash compactor bags to compression dry bags for two reasons: 1) trash compactor bags are cheap as hell, and 2) a sleeping bag in a trash compactor bag can be packed in various different positions and are much more easily packed than when in a dry sack.

Sleeping bags should never be washed. They all come with washing instructions, but it's always a mistake. Washing a sleeping bag is one of those things that *sounds* like a great idea and probably is a great idea in theory. In practice, it's all bad. If God wanted us to wash sleeping bags, then He wouldn't have given us Febreeze.

* * *

Here's an awesome tip from the road: On cold nights, rather than sliding into a freezing cold sleeping bag, it's nice to slide into a warm and cozy sleeping bag. The Walker can fill a water bottle with water that is off-boil and slide it into the sleeping bag. The water bottle will make the sleeping bag warm and cozy. Oh, Man...I'm getting nostalgic just thinking about it!

C(1)(a) Sleeping Pad

A sleeping pad is the most important piece of sleeping equipment besides a sleeping bag. A sleeping pad lifts a Walker off of the cold, cold ground. Sleeping on the cold ground will kill you with what is called *conductive heat loss*, the transfer of heat from one body to another, often larger and colder, body when the two are in contact. That's how the Earth manages to keep its core so hot—by sucking the heat from the bodies of cross-country hikers.

Sleeping pads serve another function, too: They make life on the ground just a little more comfortable.

There are two types of sleeping pads, foam and inflatable. Inflatable sleeping pads are a joke. They are ridiculous. They are not more comfortable than foam pads and they will develop leaks. You blow that sucker up and go to sleep, then you wake up shivering to death because all the air leaked out of it and you're back on the cold ground. I think that inflatable ground pads are a waste of money for a Walk.

Foam pads are the way to go. They fold up small, they are cheap, they are light, and they are comfy. Oh! You think they are less comfortable than the inflatable kind? You're wrong. They are *more* comfortable, you just are not used to it yet. Get over yourself.

D. First Aid Kit and Wilderness First Aid Education

The Walker **must** have a first aid kit. There's nothing wrong with assembling a first-aid kit, but I advise buying a pre-packaged kit because the prepackaged kind are easily identified as first aid kits. Ready-made kits come in neat, brightly colored pouches, and so are quickly identifiable in emergencies. Any old chump off the road will be able to quickly identify a pre-packaged first aid kit when they go rummaging through your pack while you're dying of malaria.

Here are a few things that your first aid kit must contain, without excuse:

47

1. Bandages and moleskin for blisters.
2. Aspirin, in case you have a heart attack. I'm not kidding. Don't take it for any other reason. But if you're having a heart attack, take aspirin. Seriously, look that up—aspirin can save your life and prevent part of your heart from dying after a heart attack. True story.
3. Ibuprofen, to fight inflammation in case of strained muscles.
4. Tincture of iodine. It hurts when applied, yes, but it doesn't hurt as bad as an infected wound that goes septic, gives you blood poisoning, and kills you.
5. Alcohol swabs to clean puncture wounds from splinters or tick bites.
6. Tweezers, for removing splinters and ticks and any other manner of things that become lodged in your skin.
7. Antihistamine, like Benadryl. Take it to prevent an allergic reaction from killing you dead.
8. Epi-Pen, if you have a severe allergy.
9. A flask of whiskey, because there ain't nothin' more olde timey and adventurous than using whiskey as an antiseptic and painkiller.

There are a hundred million other things that one *might* include in a first-aid kit. The list above is not meant to be an exhaustive list.

* * *

M.W.C. 9.2: USE SUNSCREEN.
On a related note, The Walker should always have the strongest sunscreen available and should use it liberally. This applies to any hike, whether long distance or not, and also to trips to the beach and to the market. Sunscreen should block both UV-A and UV-B rays,

and should be applied liberally to the face, the hands, and to the side of the body that is exposed to the sun. When hiking westbound in North America, it is the left side of the body that is most directly exposed to the Sun. I don't care if you're white, Indian, black, or Asian…use sunscreen. If you don't use sunscreen, you will get skin cancer and die.

M.W.C. 9: THE SUN WILL KILL YOU IF YOU ARE NOT CAREFUL; IT HAS NO EMOTIONS.

Nate Damm didn't use sunscreen on his walk, and he tells me that he has "what looks to be permanent skin damage on [his] arms as a result". I used sunscreen pretty liberally for quite a bit of the trip, and I'm not particularly fair-skinned, but I still have a few blotches on my hands. I think they are little skin cancer spots. My girlfriend says they are "age spots". What does she know? She's just a doctor. Blah.

* * *

On another related note, the Walker should always use insect/tick repellent. The controversial insect repellent DEET is the most powerful insect repellent I know of. We all know that it is bad—but walking across the country is an extenuating circumstance. The Walker is exposed to *a lot* of ticks, and so should wear a DEET-based repellent and should check him or herself for ticks *every night*. If vigilant about prevention, the Walker can usually find and remove ticks before the ticks bite.

A Walker with a dog should make sure to use Frontline or another similar product and to check the dog for ticks *every day*.

Why such a strong warning about ticks? Because Lyme disease is out there, Friend. It's out there and you get it from ticks. I know this because I had it a few years ago. And once you have it, it gets at you and causes you pain and nightmares and horrible social skills for many years.

M.W.C. 8.1: THERE ARE SOME SMALL THINGS THAT YOU SHOULD WORRY ABOUT.

In addition to Lyme disease, ticks can carry Rocky Mountain Spotted Fever, which has an untreated mortality rate around 35%. Insect repellent like DEET might be bad, but on a cross-country hike its value as tick repellent probably outweighs the negatives and the controversy.

D(1) Wilderness First Aid Training

The Walker *should* take a wilderness first aid training course prior to beginning a cross-country hike. I did not, but I got lucky. At bare minimum, The Walker should learn:

- To identify the signs and symptoms of heat exhaustion.
- To identify the signs and symptoms of dehydration.
- To identify the signs and symptoms of hyponatremia.
- To treat blisters.
- To treat allergic minor allergic reactions.
- To treat snake bites.
- To clean and to bandage wounds.
- To identify the signs and symptoms of heart attack.
- To identify the signs and symptoms of frostbite.
- To identify the signs and symptoms of trench foot.
- General methods of treating muscle strain.

Again, that is not an exhaustive list. It is merely an indication of the types of injuries that are more likely on a long hike.

The list of injuries I experienced when I walked across America includes, but is not limited to: a broken head, a broken finger, stress fractured feet, heat exhaustion, dehydration, pinched nerve, sprained ankle, several insect bites including a few ticks, sunburn, altitude sickness (or exhaustion), sciatica, gastrointestinal upset, hemorrhoids, and dehydration. Not all of these injuries were bad, but some of them were. After the Walk, I came to realize how incredibly lucky I had been during my Walk.

D(1)(a) Heat Exhaustion

The Walker will almost certainly walk through extreme heat, both in the humid Midwest and the dry heat of desert areas. By the time the Walker reaches these areas, the Walker will likely be physically able to walk many miles over long hours. For this reason, every hiker should become familiar with the signs and symptoms of heat exhaustion. Trust me: It can sneak up on you.

John Seyal says:

> "We had a really close call with heat one day—17 miles walked on a day that hit 114 degrees [Fahrenheit]. Thankfully, we knew what the signs of heat exhaustion were and took a break to cool off when we started getting delirious. If we had pushed our last mile without that break, one of us would have probably been in the hospital."
>
> --John Seyal

Now, I shouldn't speak out of turn here, but as it happens I was in telephone contact with the Seyals when they did their cross-country hike. *And,* I happened to speak with them on or about the day that he is describing. Let me say that it sounded to me at the time like it was a *hell of a lot* closer of a call than he lets on. This is why: You lose your mind with heat exhaustion and you often lose the ability to recognize that you are very near dehydration and death. It's sort of like being very, very drunk but thinking that what you *really* need is another drink.

The Seyals had the benefit of teamwork and the buddy system. One of them said something like, "Gargantuan asparagus cars are often popular vacation destinations for reformed stomach ailments", at which point the other team member said, "Whoa! Something is *not right with you!*" Then they collapsed in the shade, drank water, and slowly returned to reality. That's how I remember one of them telling the story.

I'll leave it to the reader to guess which team member suffered the perils of heat exhaustion.

Heat exhaustion and heat stroke are dangerous. The Walker should know the signs and symptoms and should not push the envelope with regard to the heat. If it's hot, especially if it's hot and humid, the Walker should probably break for a few hours during the heat of the day. Wait it out in the shade. Read a book. Talk to the locals. It's better to break for a while than to die.

M.W.C. 33: IT'S BETTER TO REST THAN TO DIE.

E. Clothes and Footwear

Oh, Man...there is nothing I detest more than "adventure clothing". I live in Chicago, where it is apparently the law that you must wear a North Face 300 weight fleece at all times. Don't know what a North Face 300 weight fleece is? Just as well. You'll learn.

Ok, here's a nitty-gritty no nonsense discussion about clothing.

E(1) Clothes

Two things above all others break the budget on a cross-country walk: clothing and lodging. Now, sometimes you can't fight the lodging costs—if it's 120 degrees and you're dying of thirst right outside a Super 8 motel, then you're going to have to make your own decision on whether to pony up for a night wrapped in the luxurious sweetness of a Super 8 bed. I had to do that once. I got stuck in a

Super 8 in rural Iowa during a "heat dome"; it was so hot that Mabel and I could hardly even leave the motel for lunch, let alone for hiking, for **8 straight days**! It was the most awful thing. So, yeah, lodging can blow your budget.

But, luckily, I'm here to help save you a couple of (hundred) dollars on your clothing budget. Like all equipment, clothes come in two categories: those you should skimp on and those you should not skimp on.

* * *

The Walker thinks of clothes in terms of layers. The base layer is that layer closest to the skin. On top of that, there are various insulating layers. Finally, there is a shell layer, which I will discuss in the subsequent section on rain jackets. The Walker's wardrobe needs to be lightweight, to take up as little space as possible, and, most importantly, to be versatile. The Walker will face cold weather, hot weather, rainy weather, humid weather, dry weather—basically every kind of weather you can imagine. So The Walker needs layers that can be added or taken away, as appropriate.

The closer to the skin, the softer and sweeter that layer should be—thus, silk sock liners, great underwear, a nice and soft thermal layer on top. In the middle, The Walker needs some insulating layers. On the outer layer—the *shell*—the Walker will need protection from rain and wind.

* * *

M.W.C. 52.1: NO COTTON.

You'll hear me say this again and again, but cotton is no friend to the Walker. Cotton is a fabric for your average, everyday pedestrian type of a person. Cotton is a fabric to put on when you're lounging. It's candy fabric; it will turn a hard man soft, and will weaken the strong will of a hardened hiker. It's not a fabric that will get you across a country on foot. So look for wool, nylon, lycra, etc.

E(1)(a) Underwear Drawz

Do not skimp on underwear.

Seriously, do not skimp on underwear.

Unlike all other clothing, underwear is near and dear to the Walker's nearest and dearest bits nearly 100% of the time on the trail, and chafing is probably the least romantic reason to end a cross-country hike. And there will be chafing.

Many hikers forego underwear. In their quest to return to the wild, to taste a state of nature, to reject the modern world, they let themselves walk *truly* free. This is ill advised. On a cross-country walk, underwear serves many important functions, but not least of which is keeping your pants clean and presentable in public. If the Walker plans to ditch modernity completely and to live out on the trail, trapping meals, eating roots, and scurrying through the forest like a lower primate, then no underwear will be necessary. But if the Walker plans to actually make it across the United States, then the Walker will have to present him or herself in public with some frequency. I don't know how to put this more delicately, so I'm just going to say it: When presenting yourself in public, it's best to not have shit and dirt and sweat all over your pants.

Wear underwear.

Underwear should be breathable, should fit snugly to prevent chafing, and (to the extent possible) should be made of some odor-controlling material.

Product Endorsement: I do not often recommend specific products, but here I recommend the Ex Oficio "Give N Go" travel underwear. These things are about $26 a pair from Ex Oficio and about $17 a pair from outlets like Campmor. And they are worth every penny. You'll likely need only two pairs. I'm not kidding! Only two pairs.

Look, I rarely spend $25 on anything, let alone a single pair of drawz. I've got whole outfits that I bought for under $15. But these underwear are amazing. They are breathable, snug but soft and comfortable, and quick drying. The manufacturer claims that they dry in about 2 hours or so, depending on humidity, and I'd say that they are selling themselves a little short—mine often dried in 2 hours or a little under even in midwestern humidity. Of all the clothing and equipment that I've ever used in my life, these were the only product about which I have never, ever had a complaint.

[*Editor's Note:* Ex Oficio did not pay the author or the publishing company to say this or in any way endorse this book or the author's Walk. That said, I will probably email them a copy of this section and see if they won't send me some clothes for free because I like free stuff and I'm broke.]

* * *

Club 3200 member John Seyal wore lightweight poly-spandex running shorts. He carried two pair. I asked him about what thoughts he had on underwear, and almost none of what he had to say is printable. This is a discussion that, as you can imagine, gets pretty nasty pretty quickly. So I'm going to paraphrase John's thoughts, cutting out each instance of his use of the word "juice", "blood", "ball", and "salt". Here we go:

> "Wear the right underwear and wash them before they get funky. That way, you won't look like you've been sitting in mud when you haven't been."
> -- John Seyal

* * *

And here's a note on chafing. It is bad and should be avoided. The Walker will almost certainly face at least one chafing experience. Boy, howdy. Now, chafing likely won't end a hike, like blisters or broken bones might. But chafing will *delay* a hike, and it won't be a pleasant delay.

My chafing experiences ended when I got those sweet Ex Oficio's that I mentioned earlier. Before that, I fought chafing primarily with Vaseline because Vaseline is cheap and has many uses.

Mr. Seyal also mentions chafing—again in colorful and passionate language. John's take on chafing is as follows:

> "I recommend a small tin of Bag Balm. Vaseline works, but Bag Balm is best. It comes in small tins that hold an ounce or two. Apply it liberally at the first signs of chafing. Don't wait until raw and bloodied and it should last for miles and miles. On my worst days, it took two or three applications over the course of the day—but it was worth every second and every ounce."
>
> --John Seyal

I'm sure Bag Balm is great. I've used Bag Balm and udder balm to soothe chafed animals before, and it's always worked great. For me, it generally wasn't worth the added expense or effort on the trail to carry bag balm because I already had a bit of Vaseline for fire starting and waterproofing. Plus, my chafing stopped by the time I hit Indiana (thankfully!). But I'll bet you that John is right: Bag Balm is probably better than Vaseline.

The important takeaway here is that the Walker should probably prepare for chafing.

E(1)(b) Long Underwear

Long underwear are a great addition in the East and again in the Rocky Mountains and West. I carried two pairs with me, which was awesome, but I only needed one. Long underwear comes in different degrees of warmth, and I had both a lighter pair for hiking and a quilted pair for sleeping. I only once had to hike wearing the heavier pair, and that was a horrible event due to weather and a bear encounter. If you're interested, check out my book *By Men or By the Earth* for the whole story in sordid detail.

The body generates a lot of heat while hiking, and sweating in cold weather can lead to hypothermia, so it is best not to overdo it with long underwear. But when sleeping, the Walker should be snug in a sleeping bag. An extra layer doesn't hurt and sure feels warm and nice on a cold night. Long underwear are light and packable, so they are a great addition. As with all other clothing worn near the body, long underwear should not be cotton.

Also, when in camp at night, and you've eaten already, and you're all snuggled up for bed wearing quilted long underwear that fit like tights, and then you get out of the tent into the cold night to get a drink of water or to look at the stars, you'll feel awesome and cool like some adventurer in a western state in the 1800s.

E(1)(c)Bottoms

The Walker can skimp here by wearing the cheapest pants that meet the minimal requirements. Again, stay away from cotton, so no jeans. Best practice is to have two pairs of hiking pants, although a Walker could get away with having a single pair if lucky enough to not have any rips, tears, or malfunctions. Two pairs allow the Walker to wear one pair until it stands up on its own and then switch to a clean pair. I recommend doing that.

Pants should be made of a quick-drying and breathable material. There are a number of nylon and poly-blend pants available, but they must be breathable. I went through four pairs of pants on my cross country hike—two were old when I started and I lost too much weight to keep them up, I replaced them with a pair of pants that I wore holes through, and I got one more pair in Nevada that I still have somewhere.

* * *

The best pants for a cross-country are convertible pants that zip off into shorts. A cross-country hike traverses several climates and several seasons. Also, you never know when you'll get a chance to live it up in a hot tub, a hot spring, or someone's pool, either—so you need to have that shorts option.

Cargo-style pants are awesome even though they make you look like a frat boy in 1998 on his way to the Dave Matthews Band concert. A vigilant shopper can find decent convertible cargo-style pants of a quick-drying and breathable material for $15 or $20 a pop, and they will be every bit as good as the $100 and $200 versions.

* * *

M.W.C. 50.1: IF YOU LOOK DIRTY, THEN PEOPLE WILL THINK YOU ARE DIRTY.

The Walker should get charcoal or navy colored pants. Light colored pants get dirty very quickly and leave the Walker looking like a dangerous homeless person. I learned this lesson the hard way.

E(1)(d) Tops

The Walker should skimp on tops as much as possible by using the cheapest tops that fit the minimum requirements.

When shopping for tops, the Walker will need to know him or her self pretty well. Pants are easy because a pair of pants and a layer of long underwear will usually be enough warmth unless it's super cold, and will usually be versatile enough to hike in warmer weather, as well. With tops, it's a whole other ball game. The human body produces heat in the upper body, so it is the upper body that must be cooled to avoid overheating, and it is the core that must be kept warm in the cold to avoid hypothermia.

Accordingly, the Walker should have multiple top layers that are as versatile as possible.

* * *

At least one layer should probably be a long-sleeve, long-underwear type shirt. These are often referred to as a "base layer" because it is the layer closest to the skin. The base layer is the least versatile layer and can be quite a pain to change in and out of when the weather changes. It should be snug to prevent chafing and to allow more layers to fit on top of it. It should be a soft material that wicks moisture away from the body, so no cotton.

The Walker should be able, at minimum, to wear the base layer with the day-to-day hiking shirt. Additionally, the Walker should be able to use the base layer when sleeping.

M.W.C. 14.2: CLOTHES SHOULD BE VERSATILE, NOT NECESSARILY EXPENSIVE.

The Walker's day-in-day-out hiking shirt should be button down, not pullover, so as to better regulate heat loss by buttoning or unbuttoning the shirt. It should have long sleeves to provide protection from the Sun. It should also be vented in the back or on the sides or both.

Above that, the Walker will need two or three additional layers. Ideally, one layer will be a long sleeve pullover that is warm but not toasty. On top of that, the Walker should have at least one heavier, warmer layer. With this set-up, the Walker will be able on the coldest hiking days to wear a base layer, a shirt, a pullover, and another insulating layer.

For me, that top, warmest layer was a cheap fleece that I got for about $12. The zippers busted on it and a mouse or something ate holes into one night in the Midwest. I replaced it with (gasp!) the ubiquitous North Face 300 weight fleece.

Now, I'm a bad example on this one, because I produce far too much body heat. I'm a freak of nature. I don't know why. My girlfriend remarks that she can feel the heat off of my body from several feet away. She thinks it's endearing. I think I probably have some sort of cancer. Whatever. The point is that I needed only the following: a hiking shirt, a pullover, and a warmer layer for lounging in camp when not hiking. I had a long sleeve thermal layer, but never wore it and ended up mailing it home.

E(1)(e) Stocking Cap and Gloves

The Walker should have a stocking cap and gloves. The only reason I didn't include these in the list of essentials is that some people might have some other form of preferred headgear and might have some sort of crazy warm pockets or something.

Cold hikes are miserable. But it is *shocking* how warm the body stays in cold weather while hiking at a brisk pace with a pack on, or pushing a cart. That said, hands are exposed and could get very cold or even frostbitten, so the Walker should have a warm pair of wool gloves. These gloves can be very cheap, but they should fit.

The same is true for stocking caps. The Walker should pick up at least one stocking cap for a couple of bucks. A stocking cap is nice to have to sleep in, as well. These can be cotton, because cotton stocking caps are so cheap.

Note that, for some reason, the Walker will see hundreds of stocking caps beside the highways. I don't know why, but people toss stocking caps out of cars a lot. If you don't mind wearing a stocking cap that has been discarded, then left beside a highway, rained on, and probably used as a makeshift home by a rat or a bird during a storm, then just pick up one when you see it and be on your way.

E(1)(f) Rain Jacket

The Walker must have a rain jacket and should not skimp on one.

The rain jacket is so important that I gave it its own heading. Some cross-country hikers take rain gear, *including rain pants*. I don't think that's necessary. Kait Seyal disagrees with me—she thinks rain pants are required gear. I disagree on that point, but everyone agrees that a rain jacket is necessary. The rain jacket should be brightly colored, as it will make the hiker more visible and less likely to be struck and killed by passing motorists. I think yellow is the best color because it provides the greatest contrast against a gray background and because people are trained to look for bright yellow as they drive. If you are on trail and you die of snakebite during a rainstorm, the yellow will help authorities find your body, too.

The rain jacket should have quality zippers that won't fail and it should be vented. Repeat: The rain jacket must have vents. Once you put the rain jacket on, it acts like a sauna. It absolutely locks in all the heat from your body and you will sweat in great amounts. Your clothes will get soaked and then you will get cold and shiver to death. Vents will help with this. You'll still die, but the vents will prolong the inevitable and help you eek out a few more miles.

Note that even fully vented rain jackets will stink after a few hours wearing them. I mean stink. It will reek like you won't believe. When I finished my hike, my roommates stole my rain jacket and washed it 20 times because it was stinking up the entire apartment. That jacket still stinks, to this day.

* * *

Now, this book includes a complete set of the most current version of the Model Walking Code (with comments). A discussion of rain jackets is a good chance to demonstrate how the individual rules of the Model Walking Code work together.

First:

M.W.C. 39: WHEN YOU NEED TO BE VISIBLE, BE VISIBLE.

Now, consider:

M.W.C. 39.1: DON'T RELY ON OTHER PEOPLE TO SEE YOU WHEN YOU NEED TO BE SEEN.

And, finally consider:

M.W.C. 27.1: FIND MULTIPLE USES FOR OBJECTS.

If you consider these rules together, it is clear that the Walker should have a brightly colored yellow rain jacket and, when the jacket is not in use, it should be stored on the outside of the pack or the cart to increase visibility.

E(2) Footwear

Feet are by far the most important equipment. Even if not hiking across America, you should care for them as if your life depends upon them, because it does. I will discuss foot care in the hygiene section, but here I will discuss best practices regarding footgear to keep the feet going out on the long, lonely, dusty, cold, rainy, populated, ugly, pretty trail.

E(2)(a) Socks

I start this footwear section with a discussion of socks because socks are more important than shoes. I know you don't believe me on this just yet, but you will.

One of the most important daily tasks on a cross-country hike is keeping feet warm and dry. If feet are not kept warm and dry, the Walker runs the risk of injury, infection, or even the dreaded trench foot. Foot injury, including blisters and infection, are likely the most common hike-ending injuries.

To keep feet warm, wear the appropriate socks. In cold weather, socks should be warm, wool socks. Cheap wool socks are not easy to find, but they are out there. As with underwear, one should not skimp on socks. All socks on the hike should be either woolen or silken, but not cotton. Again, do not wear cotton socks. Once more, no cotton socks.

M.W.C. 52.2: No cotton socks.

E(2)(a)(i) Sleeping Socks

The Walker should have one extremely warm pair of socks to sleep in, which will help keep the whole body warm while sleeping. Sleeping socks should be kept as clean as possible and the Walker should avoid hiking in them. At night, feet should be safe and healthy in clean, warm socks. Shocker: Sleeping socks can be cotton. I frown on it, but I'll allow it so long as the Walker promises to not hike a single mile in them.

I'll tell you: There are two luxury items that I would kill for on the trail: 1) tea, and 2) sleeping socks. Oh, Man, I'm having heart palpitations just thinking about this right now—hike 30 miles in cold, rainy weather, feet all banged up and sweaty and awful, then go to sleep with a full belly in a warm tent with luxurious thick, clean, sleeping socks on. Man, when you slide your howling dogs into those clean socks…it's all worth it. The world is a beautiful place.

E(2)(a)(ii) Hiking Socks

The Walker should have at least one pair of thick, warm, woolen hiking socks. These are the puffy, padded numbers that you see in sporting goods stores. If one eschews hiking boots in favor of sandals (discussed later), then he or she will likely need at least three or four pairs of these socks in order to keep feet warm and relatively clean. The Walker should always hike in the cleanest non-sleeping socks. These puffy hiking socks are kind of expensive, but they are cheaper than high tech hiking boots.

* * *

For most hiking, thinner woolen socks will do the trick. Socks should be rotated often and kept as clean as possible.

E(2)(a)(iii)Sock Liners

Two to four pairs of silk sock liners greatly improve comfort, speed, and safety on a long-distance hike. If wearing shoes and/or boots, then silk sock liners help prevent blisters better than just about anything else. I don't really get blisters, but I didn't even have a single hotspot while wearing the silk sock liners. I've spoken with many long-distance hikers who agree with me.

Silk sock liners weigh almost nothing and take up very little space, so many pairs are advisable. With more pairs, they can be rotated more frequently and will stay cleaner.

Plus, silk has interesting thermal properties. It keeps feet warm even when it is wet. I don't understand how it works. Maybe no one does—maybe it's just a miracle. Cotton is worthless when wet; wool is pretty good at holding in heat when wet; but silk is on another level. For example, on the night of the bear and the rain, my dog Mabel and I had to hike in some awful, cold, rainy weather. When we got to safety in a town, we were both shivering; I couldn't feel my hands or my legs, really, and my lips were turning blue. My feet were soaked to the bone—and still my feet were warm. Those sock liners might have saved my life that night, come to think of it.

E(2)(a)(iv) Sock Maintenance

Socks should be washed as often as is practical. Laundry is difficult on the road and is the first bit of hygiene that hikers toss out the window. So all socks should make it into the laundry at every chance. Socks should be rotated, and the Walker should try not to wear the same pair too many days in a row. The cleaner the socks, the healthier the feet.

E(2)(b) Boots/Shoes/Sandals

Ok, here's where I rail and rant against shoes and boots. But seriously, stay with me on this one.

I'm against footwear as much as possible. Everyone should do what's "best for you", but in my opinion it is best to wear as minimal footwear as possible given circumstances and conditions.

Footwear has become kind of a controversial topic in the last few years. There was even a Harvard study about running barefoot. Anyway, barefoot is all the rage these days and a bunch of people who laughed at me 5 years ago are now wearing those silly Vibram FiveFinger shoes.

When Mabel and I walked across America, I went through 5 kinds of footwear: 1) hiking boots that lasted from Delaware to San Diego, though I hardly wore them past Illinois, and which I still have; 2) a pair of tennis shoes that were awful and that I wore mostly from Primm, NV, to San Diego, CA; 3) a pair of Vibram FiveFingers that I got for free and wore for about 5 miles; 4) duct tape, that I wore for about 10 miles; and, 5) 2 pairs of Teva sandals that I hiked in exclusively for a majority of the trip from Illinois through to California.

Here's my take: While wearing shoes and/or boots, I suffered far more injuries, substantially more soreness and pain, required far more food, and made fewer miles. While in sandals, by contrast, I made better time, I had far fewer injuries, I suffered far less pain in my feet, knees, hips, and back, and I required far less food and water.

Keeping all of this in mind, here is my advice on footwear: The Walker should have a pair of shoes that are waterproof for hiking in cold, wet conditions and should make sure to have a few pairs of socks and several pairs of silk sock liners. But if hiking in good or even decent weather, sandals might be the way to go. In the summer, sandals help keep feet cooler than when in tennis shoes and provide a little bit of distance between feet and the hot pavement. Additionally, sandals require the foot to do a little more work and, in so doing, the muscles and tendons of the feet develop and become stronger, leading to fewer injuries.

Perhaps most importantly, sandals are far lighter than shoes. I've heard that some scientists determined that one pound on the foot equals eight pounds on the back. That's a big difference, but I believe it. Consider that when walking a single mile, the average person might take 2000 steps. Each extra pound in footwear then requires lifting an extra 2000 pounds over that mile, and if them thar scientists were right, then we're talking an extra 16,000 pounds for ever extra pound on the feet. Over 20 miles? That's like a million pounds.

The Walker should save those really big, heavy hiking boots for mountaineering expeditions up K2.

M.W.C. 29.3.1: SHOES WEAKEN FEET.

Before heading out on a long hike, the Walker should spend several months strengthening the feet, no matter what kind of footwear he or she plans to wear. Strengthening the feet requires spending a lot of time barefoot. Most people lead sedentary lives and have been wearing shoes for many years, so one is advised to ease gently into the barefoot lifestyle. I discuss feet training a bit more in the section on physical training.

Hike your own hike and keep your feet healthy.

E(3) Hat

A wide-brimmed hat is a necessity on a long-distance hike. The hat should have mesh venting on the top to allow ventilation in hot weather. The hat should protect the top of the head from the Sun and the brim should be as wide as possible to protect as much of the neck and shoulders from the Sun as possible.

Plus, you probably already realize that nothing looks cooler or more adventurous than a person out alone in the Great Open West with a wide-brimmed hat on. It's like a cowboy meets a fisherman meets Indiana Jones. The Walker must have a wide brimmed hat.

E(3)(i) A Note on Caps

Headgear serves two purposes for the cross-country hiker, protection against Sun and cold. You may have noticed that I put stocking caps in the same section as gloves, not in this section with hats. Why? Because I think a cap is a cap and a hat is a hat. But the important thing to remember is that a stocking cap will help prevent death from the cold and a wide-brimmed hat will help prevent death from heat exhaustion.

E(3)(ii) The Keffiyah

Ok, here's a little side note from your friendly author about the single greatest piece of road clothing ever invented: the keffiyah. For those who don't know, it's that crazy turban-looking thing that Palestinians wear. In today's mixed up world, it's a political symbol more than anything else. But all the politics around it belie the fact that it is one of the most versatile pieces of clothing I know of.

I advise, simultaneously, that the Walker should 1) carry and use a keffiyah, and 2) *not* carry and *not* use a keffiyah. Let me explain:

There are several methods of fastening the keffiyah. Depending on the way you tie the thing, it can serve as a bandana to protect your head and help keep you cool in the heat, a scarf that keeps you warm in the cold wind, a dust mask to protect your mouth and eyes from sand, a layer of cloth to help prevent your lips from chapping or burning in the sun and wind, a sun guard to protect your forehead or neck or shoulders…etcetera, etcetera. It is a phenomenally useful and versatile piece of clothing. So the Walker *should* carry and use one.

However, a keffiyah (even a plain, solid color keffiyah) makes the Walker look like an Arab. This will cause a great deal of conflict when the Walker walks through many areas of the United States. Unless you are absolutely alone and no one is around to see, you probably shouldn't walk around as a hiker wearing a turban.

That's all.

F. Electronics and 'Lectric Things

Part of the beauty and romance of a Walk is the distance you put between yourself and all of the trappings of our modern world. Phones don't ring. Emails don't ding. You fall asleep beneath the glow of stars, not the blue glow of a television. And purists will tell you that it's not a real hike if you have electronics with you. I sympathize with that notion, but I also recognize that we live in a modern world. If a Walker chooses not to take any electronics on the Walk, then I commend that. But if the Walker is going to take electronics along, perhaps consider what I have to say about it.

F(1) Light

You'll remember that I included a flashlight on the list of essentials—and I won't back down from that. The Walker will need light when pitching camp at night and often when striking camp before the Sun comes up. Against all best intentions, the Walker will invariably have to hike at night from time to time. And, often overlooked, the Walker might from time to time have to navigate long, dark tunnels. (On the C & O Canal, for example, there are a few tunnels, including the Paw Paw Tunnel, which is one of the longest unused tunnels in the world. I must have walked through 20 old train tunnels when I walked across America and I needed a flashlight in several of them.)

The best flashlights for the trail are small, are powered by about three AAA batteries, and utilize LEDs to emit light. I'm not sure any major companies make flashlights that *aren't* LED anymore—at any rate, LEDs are the way to go. These days, you can get a flashlight for about $8 or $10 that will fit in the palm of your hand and that is bright enough to see from space. I used a free flashlight that I had when the trip started, but replaced it with a Coleman hand torch that I got at Target for about $8. Of course, three days later, I found one exactly like it on the side of the road and ended up with two. I still have both and I still love them.

Rechargeable batteries are an option, but in my experience it wasn't worth the weight of the charger or the time spent near a socket. I suppose it would have been a different story if I'd had a working solar panel set up. But no matter—it's easy to find AAA batteries on the road.

The Walker should always, always, ALWAYS make sure to have at least one fresh pair of batteries as back up because batteries *will* die at the worst possible time.

* * *

One nifty trick from the road is to turn one battery around in the flashlight during the day when it's not in use. This is because hikers sometimes turn on flashlights accidentally and run the battery down. If, however, you turn one of the batteries around, then even if the push-button switch gets flipped, it's not possible to complete the circuit. So it won't turn on! It won't drain the battery! Science!

These are the kind of things you figure out on a long hike and then you become convinced that you are a genius.

* * *

A headlamp is an option. Headlamps are battery-powered LED lights mounted on an elastic band. You wear them on your head for hands-free light. They are relatively cheap these days and are relatively small and lightweight. For those reasons, I think headlamps can be a useful addition to the cross-country equipment arsenal. They are not necessary, though. The weaknesses are that they are not very bright and they burn through batteries very quickly.

* * *

One non-essential item that I really enjoyed having with me was a battery-powered lantern. It cost me about $4. It is shaped like a very small version of an old-style camp lantern, but it is powered by AAA batteries. It has a handle/hook on the top so that I could hang it in my tent, like a ceiling light. The base of it is flat, so I could also stand it up on the floor of the tent at night and read by it. I got a great deal of use out of that thing. It was light and cheap, so if a potential Walker plans on doing a lot of reading or writing at night, it is probably worth it.

F(2) Cell Phone

A phone with data services can keep a Walker connected to family and friends, to Google maps (which are invaluable), and to student loan indenture overlords. I use an iPhone in my regular life, and I used a Samsung Galaxy on my Walk; I'm happy with both. I'm not going to discuss in any more detail which type of phone or which service provider is best. They are all about the same if you ask me, so long as you know how to turn your phone on and how to use the maps. Boom. Done. Do that.

* * *

The Walker will probably come to rely pretty heavily on a cell phone. For that reason, it's important to have power on reserve. I accomplished this with a battery pack that I will discuss in a bit. It's possible, in the alternative, to carry a spare cell phone battery if your phone has easy access to the battery. I did not carry a spare battery, but I should have, because cell batteries go bad from time to time.

M.W.C. 54: IF IT'S THAT IMPORTANT, HAVE A BACKUP.

Mr. Nate Damm says: "Keep at least one extra cell phone battery with you and charged." That is great advice.

F(2)(a) Google Maps

Google Maps is an incredible service. It is *incredible*. You simply cannot believe how unimaginably amazing it is until you try to walk across a continent. With Google Maps, the Walker can get regular maps and even topographical maps so that he or she can see if there are big elevation changes coming. Google Maps can search for the nearest gas station, or the nearest hardware store. Some of the information is wrong, and often times a cross-country hike traverses large areas where there is no data service to use Google Maps. But it's invaluable when it can be used. It's amazing.

And it's freeeeeeeee!

F(2)(b) Blogging

Oh, you want to blog about your cross-country hike? You don't say! You'll probably be able to sell ads on your blog, get wicked rich endorsement deals, and eventually they'll even make a movie about you! I guess you'll need a laptop.

My advice: Skip the blog altogether. Your friends and family can keep up with you on Facebook and Twitter (and, gasp, Google+). If a hiker commits to blogging about the epic journey, then the hiker will understand the trip in these terms only: How can I write about this experience? Instead, I think the Walker should focus on this question: How can I get the most out of this experience?

Plus, no one cares.

You're probably not going to develop a massive following, probably not going to raise a million dollars for your favorite charity, and your revelatory experience is probably not going to kick start a new religion that finally brings peace and tranquility to Earth. Everyone has a blog and everyone writes about everything that happens to them—it's gotten to the point that you can't hear yourself type because everyone is typing all the time.

Seriously, in 500 years when our civilization has been wrecked, historians are going to look back and say, "Americans, as a tribe, were fascinating—they used every part of the Internet." Ridiculous.

Haven't dissuaded you? Ok, well, then I guess you'll need a laptop. Here are some suggestions:

F(2)(b)(i) Skip the laptop, take an iPad

If a Walker absolutely insists on filling the Internet with another "I'm walking across this or that or the other thing" blog, it can be done with an iPad and the WordPress app. I know, because that's what I did.

I tried to run my blog from my phone. It's not practical. If a person is serious about blogging a cross-country hike, then it's going to require at least an iPad or other tablet/netbook. The iPad is the only tablet I've ever used and I think it's quite fine, so there's that.

M.W.C. 57.1: SOME THINGS CAN BE USED FOR FREE.

There are WiFi access points all across the U.S. at motels and parks and even at gas stations in the middle of nowhere. In addition to WiFi, you can get a fairly cheap data plan on the iPad. If it makes you feel better, I guess do that. But know that the Walker will have WiFi access pretty frequently. On top of all of this, the iPad is far lighter and more compact than a laptop computer. The iPad does not charge as quickly as it could, but it charges faster than a laptop.

[*Editor's Note:* Of course, Apple didn't pay me anything to say that or give me an iPad or anything like that. I've never talked with anyone at Apple, actually. Which is a shame, because I love, love, love their iPhones and iPads and MacBooks and all their other AMADZING PRODUCTS...please, Apple, please give me free stuffffffffff.....!]

[*Author's Note:* Apple won't send me any free stuff.]

The exception: If sharing a huge number of processed, beautiful digital pictures is key to a Walk, then the Walker will have to make room in the weight budget and the dolla-dolla-bill-ya'll-budget for a laptop.

F(2)(b)(ii) Electricity

Depending on electricity needs, extra electricity storage/charging capacity might not be important. Across most of the U.S., the Walker is never very far away from electrical outlets. So unless processing a lot of photos or video, or unless the Walker is just *always* connected, Tweeting and Facebooking and blah blah blah, then the Walker can probably charge electrical equipment when near a socket. The downside to this strategy is lost hiking time while devices are charging and less versatility in emergency situations.

There are basically two options for avoiding the loss of hiking time: solar panels, or a big 'ol reserve battery. There are a number of solar panels available that can keep you charged while you're hiking. Some work well, some don't. But they all have this in common: The

Walker probably doesn't need them. I had a handy solar flap setup, too, but it didn't work and I didn't need it.

BUT WAIT! Someone disagrees with me! John Seyal walked across America in 2012 with his wife, Kait Whistler Seyal, and a couple of therapy dogs. He says:

> "I recommend solar panels, for sure. It's a good product that saved our butts every day. A small kit was enough to keep both of our cell phones charged constantly. They were the bomb and kept our stuff all charged up. Especially useful on the flat top of the pushcart."
>
> --John Seyal

See: Everyone's experience is a little bit different. The Seyals kept a great blog while they walked and took many great pictures. Their Walk was for a cause and required them to be in contact with people much more frequently than I had to be—they had to schedule therapy visits and media relations. So they know what they're talking about when it comes to keeping electrical equipment going on the road. If, like the Seyals, the Walker intends to use the Walk as a platform to raise money or awareness, that will require quite a bit more connectivity with local and national media and quite a bit more in terms of content creation for the associated blog. More connectivity plus more content equals a much higher electricity requirement.

* * *

In the absence of solar panels, a large rechargeable reserve battery that charges off a 110V socket will do the trick. (Note that functional solar panels will usually also charge these types of batteries.) A battery like this usually costs about $200. But a Walker will need it if he or she plans to change the world with a blog.

I carried a Brunton Sustain battery that ran about $150. It went to a full charge off a wall socket in about 10 hours, and a full charge would recharge my cell phone about 10 times. It came in very handy when I was stuck in a tent for several days at a time, and it came in handy a few times when I was in-between cities and needed to stay in contact with people. I was almost never so far away from mankind that I couldn't charge that Sustain battery either in a motel or in a campground.

There are power outlets all over the place. Almost all campgrounds that are not "primitive" have access to power outlets. The Walker has to stop for lunch, for a snack, or just to take a breather in the shade. While sitting there outside the Sip N Quick gas station, maybe just plug that phone in on the sly. That's #hobostyle.

M.W.C. 57.1: Some things can be used for free.

There are power outlets in municipal parks, on the outside of gas stations, behind grocery stores; there are power outlets all over the place if you just look; using these may not be "legal", in the strictest sense, but it is possible.

F(2)(b)(iii) Camera

In general, I advise people to leave most electronics at home— don't bring a computer, don't bring solar panels, don't do this and don't do that. And most smart phones have quite nice cameras built in these days, so the Walker need not bring a camera. But I *still* advise people to take a nicer digital camera, if possible. Why? Because a cross-country hike is the most amazing experience most Walkers will ever have and friends and family will want to share the experience through pictures.

And it is impossible out there to not take amazing pictures. I'm a horrible photographer and I still managed to get hundreds of breathtaking pictures. I did not have a camera with me until Montrose, Colorado, when a very nice young lady from Delaware sent me one in the mail. It was one of the nicest gifts I have ever received. She sent me a Canon PowerShot camera.

With this point and shoot camera, I was able to take pictures of far greater quality than I could with the camera built into my cell phone. Moreover, I was able to take pictures without turning on my phone and running down precious battery power on my phone. Additionally, with a 5 GB storage card, I was able to store hundreds and hundreds of pictures in the camera.

M.W.C. 41.3: AT LEAST HALF THE VALUE OF ANY GOOD EXPERIENCE IS IN SHARING IT WITH OTHERS.

To be sure, a good camera adds a lot of weight. A pretty great point and shoot is not terribly heavy, but a nice camera can get weighty pretty quickly. But, unless the Walker is a troglodyte without friends of family at all (and that's cool, too, in it's own way), then people will want to see pictures. If the Walker wants great pictures, the added weight of the camera may be justified.

> "It's impossible to recreate life on the road, but it's possible to record it. Photos and journals kept in the moment are things that I will treasure with friends and family for the rest of my life. Having photos helps me to remember the vivid details—even when it starts to get fuzzy, as if it were a dream. I carried a five-pound camera and lens with me on the entire trek, and ultralight hikers scoffed and insulted me for it. But looking back at the photos I have now, it was absolutely worth the added weight."
>
> --John Seyal

A nice camera is not necessary, and it is not lightweight, but a camera greatly enhances how accessible the trip is to friends and family. If a camera is within the Walker's budget, it's a great addition to the Walk.

* * *

M.W.C. 45: BE HUMBLE.

A Walker must be humble; a Walker must be humble before nature and before people. The Walk is an incredibly humbling experience, to the point that some Walkers become very self-aware and self-deprecating. That's a natural part of the process, I think. But this humility notwithstanding, a Walker should make sure to get pictures of him or herself during the Walk, humility notwithstanding. I didn't do this, because I am an idiot. I was alone most of the time, so it was difficult to take a picture of myself and Mabel *and* amazing scenery all in the same shot.

Here's a little support for this piece of advice: The New York Times contacted me about a year and a half after I finished walking across America. A contributor was working on a piece about cross-country hiking and they needed pictures. I sent them the four or five pictures I had with me in them, and they used one of them—it was about a quarter of a page big in the center spread of the Sunday Review. I have it framed. There's a great picture of John and Kait Seyal in the spread, too. So there you go: The Walker should try to get a few good pictures of him or herself on the trip.

F(2)(b)(iv) Kindle or e-reader of some sort

The Walker should probably carry a Kindle or an e-reader of some sort. An e-reader is not necessary, but it is pretty close. If it comes down to either a camera or a Kindle, I say go with the Kindle.

There is a huge and surprising amount of downtime on a cross-country hike. It's surprising because you think that you'll just be busy all day long, every day. It ain't like that. There are hours stuck in tents or under a shade tree in the heat. Once the Walker gets into super awesome physical shape, energy levels often go through the roof and there are many sleepless nights during that adjustment. The Walker becomes very efficient at pitching and striking camp, too, and that leads to more downtime.

There is just a hell of a lot of downtime and it can drive a person *insane* if the Walker doesn't fill that time constructively.

Reading is the best possible way to fill downtime on a cross-country hike. The Walk is an opportunity to learn, to expand consciousness, and to become better aware of the human condition—but *only* if the Walker takes advantage of the downtime. One way to do this is to fill your empty time with reading. But books are heavy! No matter: You can carry literally thousands of pounds worth of books in a single 7-ounce Kindle. If you are interested in just how much reading a person can do on a cross-country hike, check out www.tylercoulson.com and see my post listing the massive amount of literature I read during my trip.

G. Waterproofing

All electronics must be stored in waterproof containers. Waterproofing can get very expensive, especially as the number of electronics increases. The Walker should take advantage of cheap PVC bags to waterproof electronic equipment.

The camping supply company Coghlans makes heavy-duty PVC bags with splash-proof Velcro closures that are great and cheap. Specially designed waterproofing equipment can run $10 to $50 for waterproof sacks and up to $100 or more for waterproof storage boxes. Or the wise Walker could get three Coghlans PVC bags for $6. Not really a tough choice. They come in a bunch of different sizes. When I hiked across America, I packed my iPad (that someone sent to me as a gift) in a Coghlans bag. It worked like a charm and saved me about $50.

The Walker will need a small bag for the cell phone, too, because the cell phone must be stored in an easy-access location that probably won't be near the other electronics.

Then, of course, there's the iPad charger and the phone charger, so that means another bag for those. The big rechargeable batteries that I mentioned are usually marketed as waterproof, but it's such a big investment that no one should trust that piece of marketing, so there's another bag for the battery and its charger as well. Now, no one wants to run down all the power on a cell phone by listening to a hot new mix and "Walking the Walk Playlist", so that adds an iPod to the list. That's got it's own charger, so you'll need a couple waterproof sacks for those, too.

See what I'm getting at here, Folks? The wise Walker should probably leave as much of that stuff at home as possible. But no matter what electronics come along on the trip, PVC bags are the cheapest and best way to store electronics in waterproof containers.

G(1) The Umbrella

An umbrella is an essential item on a Walk. I discuss the umbrella here in this waterproofing section, although it doesn't necessarily belong here.

There is no way to get around hiking in the rain on a cross-country walk. A rain jacket is great, but an umbrella is sometimes greater. A pretty substantial part of surviving a cross-country walk is keeping dry in cold weather. So an umbrella is awesome. But it ain't the rain that makes the umbrella necessary—it's the Sun.

* * *

M.W.C. 9: THE SUN WILL KILL YOU IF YOU ARE NOT CAREFUL; IT HAS NO EMOTIONS.

What makes the umbrella *essential* is sun proofing. There is no shade between the Mississippi River and Denver (or very little). There are three trees in Nebraska, and they are all in Lincoln. The Sun is absolutely fierce in the Great Plains and in the deserts and there is no shade. It is the Sun out there that makes an umbrella necessary. The Walker should take a huge, dark, golf umbrella.

Almost everyone I know who has made a successful Walk has at some point used an oversized golf umbrella to stay out of the Sun. When stopping for a break, a hiker can use a tarp to create shade, but that takes time to pitch. The umbrella is fast, and also has the advantage that it can be used while hiking. In the deserts of Utah, for example, several days were not particularly hot except for in the direct Sun. On those days, I rigged up a way to mount my golf umbrella on my cart so that Mabel could walk in the shade.

I don't want to put too fine a point on this, but I will: An umbrella for Sun-proofing is essential and, if there is a dog out there with the Walker, it is *absolutely* essential.

G(2) Tarp

A tarp is essential. In fact, the tarp was so useful on my Walk that it even got its own Rule in the Model Walking Code. By the end of a cross-country hike, Walkers tend to have bizarre and unnatural love and admiration for the lowly tarp. I'm not kidding.

* * *

First, whether using a cart or a pack, the Walker should learn to use the tarp to cover equipment. This is accomplished with a simple square tarp—the kind with metal eyelets on the corners—and a few lengths of rope or twine. The Walker should practice wrapping equipment in the tarp early on in the Walk and should learn to do it quickly. Storms pop up sometimes with little warning, and it's important to stay on the road making miles until the absolute last minute.

M.W.C. 47.1: Preparation makes a slow job faster.

Best practice is to cut four lengths of rope or twine and affix them ahead of time to the corners of the tarp; three can be short, but one corner piece should be left pretty long. The rope is used to secure the wrapped tarp for storage and to affix the tarp over equipment. The rope can also be used to pitch the tarp as a shade in the West by fixing the corners to trees, rocks, etc.

* * *

The Walker should wrap equipment *every night* until the other side of the Rocky Mountains. From February on the East Coast through to the Rocky Mountains in summer, nighttime can bring surprise rain. Even when it doesn't rain, dew often forms on equipment that is left unprotected. The tarp will help mitigate wetness (and damage) from dew.

M.W.C. 27.1: Find multiple uses for things.

When camped near picnic tables, the table is the best place to store equipment at night. The fastest and easiest method of tenting near a picnic table is to store equipment on top of the picnic table at night and use the table to secure the tarp over the equipment.

* * *

M.W.C. 24: Always have quick access to your tarp.

The Walker should always store the tarp on the outside of the pack or near the opening/on the outside of any pushcart. It should be the easiest thing to access. I always kept my tarp tied to the outside of my pack so that I could access it quickly. This came in handy numerous times when rain blew in.

When stopping for breaks (which every Walker should do), the tarp makes a quick seating area. It helps keep clothes clean and dry, especially if the ground is moist, and it helps a little to keep ticks and other critters on the dirty ground where they belong.

* * *

In the desert, where it is almost certainly not going to rain, but where campsites tend to be rocky, the tarp makes a great makeshift footprint to protect the floor of the tent. Earlier, I advised against buying an overpriced "footprint" for the tent. I advise this because a footprint is probably not necessary for most of a cross-country trip. In the dry western states, the use of a thick tarp to protect the tent became arguably useful. By the time the Walker reaches the western states, rain ain't usually a big danger. In those instances, the tarp makes a great footprint.

When using a tarp as a footprint, fold the extra material *under* the tarp itself so that the tarp is roughly the same size as your tent's floor. If you leave extra material around the tent, the tarp might act like a basin, collecting moisture all night long until you wake up in two inches of water. No one wants that.

G(3) Clothes and Sleeping Bag Should Stay Dry

The Walker must keep clothes and sleeping bags dry. There are other things to be kept dry, too, like food.

Here's some trail wisdom that can save a ton of money. There are two options to keep this stuff dry: either spend a ton of money on "dry sacks", which are very high-tech selectively permeable bags with fold-over closures, or use trash compactor bags.

M.W.C. 22: SAVE MONEY, ALWAYS.

Trash compactor bags are much thicker and more durable than regular trash bags and will keep clothes, sleeping bag, and food dry. I bought one box of trash compactor bags in Maryland or Ohio and had more than enough to last me all the way to California. Every now and again, I even threw out an old trash compactor bag that was perfectly fine just to use a new one. That box of trash compactor bags cost me about $8 and within days had replaced two extremely expensive dry stuff-sacks.

H. Self Defense

The two most common questions that people ask a potential Walker are: 1) Why are you doing this?, and 2) Are you taking a gun? Now, gun control is quite a controversial topic. But for the Walker, there is no controversy at all: **Do not take a firearm on your cross-country hike.**

H(I) Guns

People put immense pressure on potential Walkers to carry a gun. Many people shake their head and say, "Well, I sure would take a gun if I were you!" But here's the thing: They aren't you; if they were, maybe they would be walking across the country in the first place instead of explaining why it can't be done without a gun. They are wrong.

M.W.C. 49.1: A (WO)MAN AIN'T NO (WO)MAN IF (S)HE CAN'T WALK ACROSS A CONTINENT WITHOUT A GUN.

Here's a table of some of the pros and cons I've identified about carrying a gun on a cross-country hike:

Cons	Pros
--Greatly increases chances of accidentally shooting yourself in your tent, or someone else. --You will likely be harassed by police and arrested or your gun taken from you. --You will not be welcomed in people's yards or homes. --You will not be welcomed in motels or campgrounds. --You will not be welcomed in National Parks. --You will have to carry an extra twenty pounds of gun and ammunition for no reason whatsoever.	--You will be able to rise up and defend your civil rights against the invading Red Army by taking to the hills, shooting reindeer for food and clothing, and saving the American way of life by re-conquering and occupying your hometown

Look, a person can't go walking around with a rifle slung over the shoulder. If you want to, be my guest, but you'll have a hell of a time walking through a town without being harassed or arrested. You can't leave a rifle lying around while you're away from your gear. You can't take your gun with you into the shower, etc. Same goes for a handgun. If you carry one in your pack or your cart, it will do you no good because you won't be able to retrieve it "when you need it" (although you will never need it). And if you want to holster up and go roaming around like Wyatt Earp, then, again, be my guest. But you'll look like a fool and you won't have a great time.

I like guns, Man. I'm a gun guy. But the Walker just doesn't need one. It will cause a ton of problems and will not solve anything.

M.W.C. 49.2: IF YOU'RE AFRAID TO WALK ACROSS THE COUNTRY WITHOUT A GUN, STAY AT HOME.

H(2) Bear Spray

The Walker should carry bear spray.

Bear spray is a bit expensive (but way cheaper than a gun), but it could mean the difference between life and death. The Walker should keep a can of bear spray with him or her at all times, including in the tent at night. Bear spray is one of the things that should be included in the "tent sack" that I will explain to you later.

Bears will kill you. They are ferocious. Each bear weighs as much as two other bears and eats four times as much. Bears represent mathematically impossible danger. Each year, 1000 people are stalked by grizzly bears and murdered in their beds in their homes. Black bears hunt humans as well, though they usually do not kill; they usually approach cautiously and sucker old people into buying lifetime annuities.

Bears are a threat, but nothing to get too worked up about. I humbled the hell out of a black bear in Maryland, and I'm a pansy, so what's that say about the state of black bears? Grizzly bears are another matter, of course. They will kill you. But a can of bear spray, when properly used, can stop a charging grizzly. Think about that! That's a powerful can of pepper spray.

You know what else bear spray will stop in its tracks? Yup.

Here's what Nate Damm has to say:

"Don't just wait until you think you need bear spray and procrastinate about getting it. Get it immediately, because you'll really regret not having it when a bear is charging full speed at you and you have no way to protect yourself."
--Nate Damm

And if you're wondering "What the Hell does Nate Damm know about charging bears?", then let me tell you something. In Colorado, a bear charged out of the woods toward young Mr. Damm. The bear would have killed him, cut his body into filets, marinated him, then roasted him and fed bits of him to his bear friends at their Super Bowl party were it not for the fact that the bear got distracted by a herd of deer and went after them. Or at least that's the story he tells. It's not like he has proof, or anything. Except, of course, for THE PICTURE HE TOOK OF THE BEAR CHARGING HIM.

I carried two 10.2 oz cans of Counter Assault bear spray. It costs about $50 a can. Only one can is necessary, but I got a deal on the second can. These cans of bear spray will shoot for about 10 seconds and over almost 30 feet. It's a serious weapon.

If you ever have to use it, try not to fire it into the wind. That will ruin your day.

* * *

M.W.C. 42.1: YOUR ACTIONS AND INACTIONS AFFECT OTHER PEOPLE.

A note on camping in bear country:

When in bear country, always 1) use a bear bag or bear canister, and 2) ALWAYS clean up after yourself. Never leave trash behind, even if it's just an "empty" can of beans or a half-eaten Snickers bar. Never leave trash in fire pits. Carry it all out to a bear-proof trashcan. These practices are non-negotiable.

The Walker pretty quickly realizes that, even though we are each individually very small and insignificant, our individual actions impact the lives of other people. In this case, poor backcountry stewardship like leaving trash around causes bears to become accustomed to human trash. They lose their fear of humans and then you have a problem bear. So the Walker must do everything practical to clean up trash when in bear country.

Also, never camp near trash cans in bear country. If you do, you'll die.

H(3) Hiking Stick

Best practice for a Walker is to carry a stout hiking stick. There are many reasons for this. I mention it in the self-defense section because a quality, stout walking stick is a pretty powerful deterrent against criminals and na'er-do-well types. A Walker carrying a stout walking stick is far less likely to be harassed or assaulted. Plus you look a little like Moses, and that's cool.

A stout hiking stick allows a person to put distance between him or her self and wild dogs—and there will be wild dogs. A stick allows a person to put some distance between him or her self and black bears, should any amble into camp. It generally aids in ongoing negotiations with all wildlife that is not of the mountain lion variety. (Nothing will help you with a mountain lion. A stick won't keep mountain lions away, and they'll set upon you long before you can get the bear spray out of your holster and take the safety off. They are silent, fierce, and obscenely strong. Mountain lions are fueled by a profane bloodlust and will kill you at every opportunity. They are majestic creatures.)

Perhaps most importantly, a stout walking stick can be applied to the cranium of indigenous primates who might seek to harm a good-natured Walker. In the event that a primate becomes aggressive, the options are to be beaten senseless and robbed of all belongings, or to employ reciprocal "negative negotiation tactics". These tactics include application of bear spray to the face of the offending primate, and/or the repeated application of a stout walking stick to the head and neck of the primate. Regardless of which method is employed, it is best practice to subdue the aggressive primate and then to run like hell. Remember that you're a stranger in their land. They probably have friends there.

* * *

And a quick word on trekking poles: Trekking poles are stupid. Take a second and look at some guy walking around with trekking poles. Now tell me seriously—do those people look stupid? Yes, they do. Trekking poles are a waste of money because they accomplish the same primary task that a stout hiking stick does, but are more expensive, they make you look like a poncing fool, and they completely fail to accomplish the other task that a hiking stick should accomplish: Head smacking.

I. Stove and Cookwear

The Walker should carry a pot to cook in and some sort of cook stove. There are hundreds of camp stove options. For a Walk, the best options are simple, light, and cheap.

* * *

First, only one pot is required. Some folks set out on cross-country hikes with two pots and a small frying pan. (I did.) That is crazy. The Walker cooks and eats from the same pot.

Backpacking pots come in various materials and sizes. Some are quite expensive. Best practice is a 1.5 or 2-liter metal pot with a lid. The MSR company sells a two-pot stainless steel set for $50 and a two-pot titanium set for about $140. Titanium is lighter and stronger than steel, but in my opinion it is not worth the extra cost. A single stainless steel pot is light enough.

The pot should be strong enough to not get bent and banged up, but as thin as possible. It should be thin because thicker pot walls take longer to heat up, which means more fuel and longer cook times. It should be large enough that the Walker can store the stove inside the pot when hiking. In my opinion, stainless steel is fine—titanium is better, but it's not worth the extra cost.

I had an MSR "alpine" cook set that came with two stainless steel pots. I needed only one and soon sent the second one home in the mail. It was an important lesson in minimalist living.

* * *

There are a thousand options when it comes to camp stoves, and each hiker has his or her preferred type of stove and fuel. For the Walk, best practice is usually a cheap, light alcohol stove.

A stove is not actually *essential* on a Walk because many meals do not require cooking, and cooking can be done on open fires. However, open fires for cooking are surprisingly rare on a Walk. Most campsites on a Walk don't allow fires (or would betray your location, in the case of stealth camping) and the Walker rarely has the energy or time to gather enough wood fuel to build a fire, anyway. So a stove, while not *essential*, is best practice.

There are basically four types of camp stoves. They are: 1) gasoline/kerosene/white fuel stoves, 2) alcohol stoves, 3) specialized wood stoves, and 4) specialized fuel stoves. I'll take these in reverse order.

Some people love specialized fuel stoves. These are little stoves that run on specifically designed fuel pellets or liquid fuel. Many also come integrated with a specially designed cook pot. These things are wonderful for a 3-day backcountry hike, or even a 10-day hike.

Forget about these things for a cross-country hike, though—they are expensive and specialized fuel is difficult to find.

Specialized wood stoves are fancy little numbers that burn wood fuel (which are twigs and leaves and what not) but these highly engineered stoves produce a lot of heat with little fuel. Most require a few batteries to run a fan. These are great, but much can go wrong with them and many times there is no access to wood fuel.

SO! Alcohol stoves. These are the way to go. An alcohol stove is a little aluminum pot. You pour alcohol into it and light the alcohol on fire. You can build alcohol stoves out of pop cans if you'd like, but I wouldn't recommend it because you can buy nice manufactured alcohol stoves cheaply. If you build one, remember that you'll also have to build a stout pot stand and a windscreen, but those items generally come packed with a manufactured stove.

Alcohol burns cooler than gasoline or wood, so boiling time is slower, but an alcohol stove will boil a quart of water in about 9 minutes (I'm basing most of this discussion on my Etowah II stove) compared to a shorter time for gasoline stove. The time lost there is more than made up by the time saved in setting up and cleaning an alcohol stove—it sets up in seconds compared with a couple of minutes for a gasoline stove.

Alcohol stoves are very light; mine weighs about 4 oz, compared to a couple of pounds for a gasoline stove. Alcohol stoves are very simple, and almost nothing can go wrong with them. Fuel is very easy to find: Alcohol stoves run on denatured alcohol, which is what you find in yellow bottles of fuel-line antifreeze, like HEET. (You can also use the red bottles of HEET or even rubbing alcohol, but both of those burn much cooler and dirtier and will leave all of your cooking equipment covered in soot.) Lastly, and this is a big, big plus, you can carry denatured alcohol around in plastic bottles like soda bottles. Gasoline must be stored in metal storage bottles, by contrast, and that adds weight.

The Etowah II stove set me back about $15. And there are a bunch of similarly priced little alcohol stoves on the market.

M.W.C. 25.1: The simpler, the fewer things will go wrong.

A few words of caution are necessary for an alcohol stove, though: The Walker should read the instructions and warnings. When alcohol burns, the flame is blue and sometimes difficult to see, so it is sometimes difficult to tell if the thing is burning or not. That can be dangerous because alcohol stoves are open-fire stoves and you should never add fuel to a burning alcohol stove. They also take a while to cool down, so it's best to give them a while to cool down after using.

Although alcohol stoves are the best option for 90% of a cross-country hike, gasoline stoves are a decent choice, too. There may be situations on a Walk in which an alcohol stove might not work—at high elevation, for example, or in extremely cold weather, or if cooking for many people. It is only in these rare situations that a gasoline stove might be worth the extra time, money, and weight.

Gasoline stoves are what most people think of when they think of a camping stove. Most have a triangular pot stand with a wick and burner in the middle, and a fuel line runs off to the side to a bottle of fuel that is pressurized by pumping air into it. Some are fuel specific and will run only on gasoline, or only with white fuel, or only with kerosene. If a Walker decides to go this route, it's best to pony up the extra five or ten dollars and get a multi-fuel stove that can burn any of those types of fuel.

These things burn as hot as blue blazes and will boil a quart of water just about as fast as you can imagine. They sound like jet engines. Plus, they continue to burn hot and long even at high altitudes and in cold weather. Gasoline is readily available and a 20 oz can of gasoline will last a single Walker for a long time.

The problems: These stoves are heavy, expensive (at around $100 plus the cost of a gas canister), and frequently require repair work. These are a bad choice for Walkers who are uncomfortable performing maintenance like changing wicks or clearing fuel lines.

The Walker should have some way of cooking, but about 85% of meals on a cross-country hike consist of food that doesn't need to be cooked.

J. Fire

A Walker should carry two forms of fire-starting tools and know how to build a fire. A properly prepared Walker will not need a fire, even on cold nights. Still, there is nothing that warms a body up like sitting beside a fire after a cold day on the trail. Moreover, if an emergency were to arise—for example, if a Walker or hiking partner were injured and needed to keep warm or to signal for rescue—a fire could save a life.

First, the cigarette lighter. Put all your macho "I am man, I start fire with stick" mumbo jumbo on the shelf. There is no better way to start a fire than with a cigarette lighter. They are cheap and available at any gas station. I had at least two on me at all times when I walked across the U.S. The Walker should buy a pack of five or eight lighters, put one in a front pocket, one in a fire bag (discussed later), one in the tent bag, etc. Lighters should be all over the place and easy to access.

Secondly, I recommend a magnesium fire striker. These cost about a buck and will light about a thousand fires. A magnesium fire striker is a block of magnesium with a flint striker built into one side. You shave off flakes of magnesium with your knife onto some tinder, and then you strike sparks onto the magnesium flakes using the back of the knife or other metal. These things work like a charm. I even started a fire in the rain with one once.

K. Bear Bag and/or Bear Barrel

In the East, then again in the West, the Walker must take precautions against bears. The two most widely used pieces of bear protection equipment are the bear bag and the bear barrel. Best practice is to use a bear bag when camping in bear country, but to use a bear barrel in certain areas (like Rocky Mountain Park) where bears have learned to search for bear bags.

* * *

A bear bag is exactly what it sounds a like: a bag that is used to hang all food and scented toiletries in a tree. High tech bear bags cost about $25, but I bet you know what I think about those…. Any old bag that is made of a lightweight material will do. It should be waterproof, but that can be accomplished with the addition of a trash compactor bag. The high tech bear bags are claimed to be scent proof and, if true, then maybe they would be worth the extra expense. However, I don't believe that they are scent proof. So any old bag can work. In addition, the bear bag requires a long length of parachute cord. (I discuss hanging a bear bag below.)

Best practice is to put all food and all scented items in the bag and hang it in a tree several hundred yards *downwind* from the campsite. "All scented items" includes toiletries, some medicines, mints, etc.

Bear barrels are marginally better at locking in scents, but are heavy and more expensive. A bear barrel is a thick plastic barrel with a locking top. These could be hung in a tree, as well, but it's not required. With a bear barrel, all food and scented items are put into the barrel, the barrel is locked, and is left a couple hundred yards downwind from the campsite. The only upside that I really experienced from my bear barrel was that it could double as a stool for sitting on in the middle of the day.

But note that some places require the use of bear barrels. In Rocky Mountain Park, for instance, you can't camp without a bear barrel. Them's the rules. This is because bears in some areas have become accustomed to bear bags there and will tear them down.

Bear barrels are expensive. There's no way around that. A decent sized bear barrel will be heavy and will cost about $80.

L. Knife/Multi-tool

The Walker must carry a knife. But *everyone* should carry a small knife with them at all times because the knife is the coolest, most useful, most versatile tool in the history of mankind.

M.W.C. 19.1: EVERYONE SHOULD CARRY A SMALL KNIFE WITH THEM AT ALL TIMES.

While walking across America, I used a knife to do a million things including, but not limited to: opening packaging, cutting twine/rope, shaving, cleaning wounds, applying butter to bread, digging out the head of a tick, feathering out damp sticks to make kindling, and loosening/tightening regular-head screws. Get a knife!

The general equipment rule is to go cheap and go light, but both of these rules can be bent in favor of a multi-tool. I got a Leatherman multi-tool because its utility outweighed its weight and cost. My Leatherman tool included a flat head and Phillips head screwdriver, file, saw, knife, cuticle scissors, ruler, awl, and can opener. Most importantly, it opened up into a pair of needle-nosed pliers and wire cutters.

I am not going to tell you why wire cutters might come in handy. I won't tell you here, and I won't tell you in the stealth camping section. I will never, ever tell you that wire cutters can be used to cut through a chain-link fence. This is something that I would never say about wire cutters or Leatherman multi-tools.

Plus, it came in a leather holster that fit on my belt. It looked stupid as hell, but it was convenient. The multi-tool was probably my third most used piece of equipment, after the walking stick and the tarp.

UPDATE: Upon returning to Chicago, I used the Leatherman multi-tool to apply peanut butter to a bagel one day and subsequently lost it. I have no idea where it is. If the Leatherman company would like to send me a free one, that would be great!

I'm so broke.

One more step. One more step. One more step. One more step. One more step. One more step. One more step. One more step. One more step. One more step. One more step. One more step. One more step. One more step. One more step. One more step. One more step. One more step. One more step. One more step. One more step. One more step. One more step. One more step. One more step. One more step.

V. Training

M.W.C. 29.3 Strengthen the weakest parts.

A Walker should try to get into decent shape before beginning a cross-country hike. I did not, because I am an idiot. But now Walkers have the benefit of learning from my mistakes.

We're pretty sedentary as a culture. Many of us spend our days behind a desk, dreaming of getting away from daily grind, getting out into the world. These sedentary folks want to be a part of it, to feel sunlight and wind, to prove that they have a timeless, evolutionary value buried inside them. It's screaming to get out. They want adventure. But even more than adventure, they want freedom.

FREEDOM!

Problem: We're fat and lazy.

The bad news is that we should all get into better shape with a little training. The great news is that all the necessary training is freeeeee!

Let me recap a few of the things that I experienced that would have been avoided had I done the proper training ahead of time:

1. My feet swelled to the size of footballs every night for a month; I'm fairly certain both feet had stress fractures.
2. I fell and broke my head and a finger, largely because I was not in good shape.
3. I "broke" an ankle, an injury that plagues me to this day.
4. I was certain I was having a heart attack most of each day for two weeks.
5. On three different mornings I woke up so sore that I could not stand up. (Not an exaggeration. I could not stand up

and had to lie there for a few hours until my back stopped seizing.)

6.   I got sciatica. That's a syndrome that only old men who wear house slippers should get, but I got it, mostly because I didn't prepare my flexibility ahead of time.

7.   I nearly died twice of exhaustion, once in West Virginia and once in Colorado. The first time was because I was not adequately prepared for the hike, the second because…well, that's a long story.

I experienced a lot of pain and suffering that I could have avoided had I just done the proper training. So here is what I learned that I *should* have done before I did my Walk.

A. Physical Training

No one should attempt a cross-country hike if not physically able to do so. Everyone should see a doctor before beginning anything as mind bogglingly stupid as walking from coast-to-coast. It is very demanding. I didn't see a doctor before I did it. Don't be like me. Be a thinker. Go see a doctor. I'll wait here….

Ok, the Doc gave you the all clear?

Well, then, let's talk physical training. This section discusses some of the information and tools necessary to design a training regiment.

Training for a Walk should consist of two overarching subjects, flexibility and strength, and should focus on the following things, in descending order of importance: 1) flexibility, 2) foot strength, 3) core and lower back strength, and 4) shoulder strength (if carrying a pack). You'll notice that I did not mention walking in that list. That's a shocker, I know, but bear with me on this one. Focus should be first on flexibility, as flexibility training will also improve overall strength and health, and second on building strength in the three key areas of feet, core, and shoulders.

B. Flexibility

The Walker should do yoga.

I know, I know, yoga is stupid. Acclaimed German filmmaker Werner Herzog calls yoga classes "abominations", and I somewhat agree with him. However, Werner Herzog's longest hike was like 400 miles, so what the hell does he know, right? Right.

Yoga is great. The Walker should begin a yoga training routine as soon as possible (after consulting a physician, of course). Potential Walkers can learn yoga from books, YouTube, classes, or whatever. If a Walker can't get beyond all the "yoga stuff", the "Namaste" and spiritual stuff, then that Walker should at least do lots and lots of stretching. The stretching/breathing practice of yoga is beneficial with or without all of the spirituality stuff that comes along with yoga. Yoga will change your life—I'm not kidding about that.

Stretching should focus on flexibility in the calves, the hamstrings, the lower back, and chest. (Yes, the chest—it was a surprise to me, too.) The Walker should stretch these bits every day. If a person cannot touch his or her toes, that person should put off a Walk until he or she can do so.

I think that the lower back and chest stretches should incorporate some of yoga's twisting positions, as this will build strength for the dangerous twisting maneuvers required to put on and take off a heavy pack. Anyone can find YouTube videos demonstrating these twisting positions and mimic them, but anyone doing so should take care not to over exert or hurt him or her self. Yoga is some serious business and you should fear and respect it.

* * *

If a training regiment consists of nothing else, it should at least require the Walker to learn how to squat properly and to spend a lot of time in a full squat position. The insensitively named "third world squat" is probably the best single exercise to prepare for a cross-country hike. This stretch requires keeping both the heels and the balls of the feet on the floor and squatting as low as possible, into a resting position. Once able to do a full squat, the Walker should spend some time in that position—I mean like ten, fifteen minutes at a time. It stretches the hips, the lower back, calves, and shoulders.

M.W.C. 29.2: LEARN TO DO A FULL SQUAT.

No one should attempt to walk across the United States unless that person is able to do a full squat. The Walker will need to be able to squat, if you know what I'm saying.

C. Foot Training

The Walker should train his or her feet before beginning a Walk. You're thinking, "Wait…can I *train* my feet?" Yes, you can…sort of.

M.W.C. 29.3.1 SHOES WEAKEN FEET.

Prior to beginning a Walk, a transcontinental hopeful should strengthen his or her feet by maximizing time spent barefoot. Never wear shoes when at home. Do you work in an office? Great! Stand barefoot or sock footed at your desk. Can't afford a stand-up desk? Who cares! Stack up a bunch of papers or a box on top of your desk and put your computer on top. Boom! Stand-up desk. I did this when I worked at a huge, glitzy law firm, and it was one of the few things I did right in terms of training for my Walk across America.

People who are already walkers or runners should incorporate barefoot walking/running into their existing training. This should be done slowly and cautiously because it can lead to injury if hurried. Calves and ankles should be stretched after each workout. (Whether to stretch before a workout is subject to some debate and, as in all things, transcontinental hopefuls should consult a physician before starting or altering any training.)

It is also best practice to wear flat-soled shoes. If the heel of a shoe's sole is thicker than the front toe-end of the sole, it is called a "positive heel". If the sole is the same thickness front to back, then it is a flat sole. The positive heel is one of the worst inventions in the history of mankind. (Indeed, most everything about modern footwear is horrible and stupid.) Positive heel shoes unnaturally shorten the calf muscles and tendons, leading to tightness in the ankles and injury. Flat-soled shoes, by contrast, allow the calf to remain at its full length when standing or walking. For this reason, flat-soled shoes are better for Walkers.

But, of course, everyone should go see a doctor and a podiatrist before beginning any Walk or training program.

Feet are the first thing to give out each day at the beginning of a Walk, so the stronger the feet and ankles, the longer the days at the beginning of a Walk.

D. Core/Lower Back Training

The Walker should also strengthen the lower back and core.

To the extent possible, lower back training should incorporate twisting motions and twisting stretches, especially if the Walker intends to carry a pack. This is because putting on and taking off a heavily loaded pack is quite stressful on the lower back. I would guess that a pretty high percentage of backpacking injuries occur when putting on or taking off a heavy pack. It takes lower back and core strength to put on a pack correctly and, even if the lower back is weak, it may be subject to strain when engaged in this unnatural motion. Twisting stretches might help prevent injury in these instances. Note, however, that twisting exercises are dangerous and should only be done with proper instruction.

Core strengthening is important because the core, along with the glutes, keep we upright primates walking upright. For practical core strengthening, the Walker should probably focus on plank exercises.

Plank exercises are especially useful, as they strengthen the core and the shoulders simultaneously. The core and the shoulders work as a team when hiking. Leg lifts and leg raises are also helpful. The Walker should not bother so much with crunches or sit-ups, as these might anger the lower back and are not super-helpful with hiking.

E. Shoulders

And speaking of shoulders…. The Walker should do as much as possible to strengthen the shoulders, upper back, and chest. This can be done with body weight exercises like push-ups and pull-ups. Push-ups should be done as much as possible in the months leading up to the Walk. Shoulder shrugs are also invaluable in preparing the shoulders to bear the weight of a pack. Shoulder presses are helpful, as are deltoid flys. Note that shrugs and deltoid flys are useful even if done without any weight.

As with every other part of the body, stretching and flexibility in the shoulders should be priority one.

My shoulders killed me at the beginning of my Walk, and I have fairly strong shoulders. I could have avoided all that pain had I just spent a little more time preparing them.

F. Walking

As strange as it sounds, walking is not an integral part of a pre-Walk training regiment.

This is counter-intuitive, I know. But the thing to remember is that the human body has been designed by a million years of evolution to walk, so as long as a person is *able* to walk, he or she will likely be quite good at it. The body gets in shape for walking very quickly, and the early days of a Walk can act as training days.

Walking is not at all like push-ups, for example. If you can do only five sets of five push-ups on a Monday, then you aren't going to be able to do five sets of 50 push-ups on Friday, even if you train very hard all week. But if you can walk only one mile on a Monday, but you get out there and walk every day and push pretty hard, then you'll probably be at ten miles a day in under a week, or just a little over. From there it's a hop, skip, and a jump to 20 miles a day. Once you hit 30 miles a day, well, then you're on your own. Everyone's body works differently once you get into the high mileage days.

G. To Train or Not to Train: A Case Study

During my cross-country hike, quite a few people reached out to me for advice. I was pretty sure that most of them would never get to the starting line. But I could tell that John and Kait Seyal were pretty serious about it. I met with them before they began their trip and I gave them basically the same sage wisdom discussed above. They started their hike about ten months later. And they made it! So here's what Kait has to say about training:

"There are two basic schools of thought: train and don't train. Surprisingly, I'm not going to say that one is better than the other. It comes back to "knowing yourself". If you have been sedentary in the past several years, then it is probably in your best interest to start building a more mutually beneficial relationship with your body. I don't believe that physical training can do any harm, assuming you are responsible about it. Being stronger is always a good thing."

[*Editor's Note:* Consult a physical before beginning *any* training program.]

"John and I did not train. We had never been on a hike of more than an afternoon or two before this. We did a bit of what we called "stress-testing". We took several long walks to find out if we could walk 10, 15, and then 21 miles a day. We needed to see if our dogs could do it, too, while we were still in a familiar environment and able to call for a pick up in the event of a…learning experience.

"We also ditched our shoes and started building up the oh-so-little but important muscles, ligaments, and tendons in our feet. This training was subtle and a little *dirty-hippy*, but paid big dividends in the long run.

"We hit the road in Delaware a couple of soft, skinny, pale little children playing like we were going to walk across a continent. And we hurt. Everywhere. We cursed Nate Damm and Tyler Coulson because both had told us not to bother walking too much—"The road will whip you into shape soon enough," they said. But we learned something in retrospect. Because we were so painfully aware of how our little bodies were not ready to hit the ground flying at 20+ miles a day, we took our time. We didn't expect too much from our bodies because we hadn't really warned our bodies what was coming. We were patient. We processed the pain into what it told us about our weaknesses and about how we were carrying ourselves. We slowly got stronger and picked up speed over the first month or so until we hit our 20+ mile stride. This may have been one of the most gratifying experiences of the whole trip."

--Kait Whistler Seyal

Kait's a wise person.

So it looks like four out of four cross-country hikers more-or-less agree: Pre-Walk training should focus on feet, shoulders, and core.

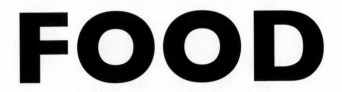

VI. Food

M.W.C. 29.1 Eat good food; don't eat garbage.

There is no "right" way to eat. Everyone's metabolism is unique, so what works for one person might not work for another. A cross-country hiker ends up doing quite a bit of experimentation in this area.

Getting enough calories on the road can be difficult, and I would advise anyone with special dietary restrictions to not attempt a cross-country hike. For example, I imagine that a severe allergy to wheat or peanuts would be a logistical nightmare. I hardly eat any wheat or peanuts in my regular life, but both were staples for me on the road. Any special dietary consideration, from allergies to diabetes, will increase the difficulty and danger of a cross-country hike.

Remember that some folks might have special dietary considerations that *they don't yet know about.* So, as with training, make sure to visit a physician before considering something so crazy as a cross-country hike.

* * *

As a first cut, the Walker should begin paying close attention to what the body is saying at the beginning of the hike. No matter how well you think you know your body, you will be in for a few surprises. By a month or so into the trip, the Walker should have a good idea of how much and how often he or she has to eat. For me, the secret was to eat high-energy foods in small quantities all day long. I literally walked and ate all the way across the country. Some people might get by with a breakfast and a dinner—but not me.

The Walker burns several thousand extra calories per day, and soon enough begins to understand food in elemental terms: carbs, fats, straight sugar, protein, and salt. At some point, the Walker will crave each of these things individually and powerfully. Everyone who walks across the United States becomes obsessed with both calories-per-dollar and calories-per-gram of food—the Walker wants cheap, light food that is loaded with calories.

* * *

A Walker should always carry enough food for emergencies. Best practice is to estimate how many calories would be necessary in an emergency to either 1) hike out of danger, or 2) keep your wits about you while you wait to find help. The Walker should carry at least that much food at all times.

A. The Sad Gas Station Truth

The sad truth is that most cross-country hikes end up fueled mostly by gas station food. When cross-country hikers get together and talk about the experience, someone invariably mentions that it's like "living gas station to gas station". As in life, a successful Walk requires a great deal of time management, and an easy way to save time and energy is to cut down on food prep time. Unfortunately, this is often accomplished by eating nasty food from gas stations.

The Walker should do everything possible to avoid using gas stations as the primary source of food on a Walk.

* * *

The easiest way to avoid using gas stations as a quick and easy source of fast calories is to carry fast, easy, high calorie food. The best source of easy, calorie dense food that I found was simple: nuts, seeds, and fruit.

That might be a problem for people with nut allergies.

B. Trail Mix—the Hardcore Trail Food

Trail mix is the greatest trail food of all time. There is no lighter way to carry so many good calories and no better way to get a healthy mixture of carbohydrates, fats, and protein while on an adventure. You can buy packaged trail mix or, like me, you can build your own and save money. Here's what you need:

Nuts, seeds, dried fruit. Feel free to add some chocolate if you'd like, but you don't need to. Put it all in a big zip-loc bag and you've got yourself some hardcore trail food.

My go-to recipe is peanuts/raisins, almonds, walnuts, banana chips, and dried apricots. That list is in descending order of quantity, so it's almost equal amounts of peanuts and raisins, but slightly fewer raisins than peanuts, fewer almonds than raisins, fewer walnuts than almonds, fewer banana chips than walnuts, and fewer dried apricots than banana chips. Sometimes I add sunflower seed kernels.

I don't know about anyone else, but I could probably live on trail mix alone and be relatively happy with my lot in life.

C. Hot Meals

A hot meal is one of the nicest things in life. But the truth is that I had almost entirely stopped cooking by the time I reached Nebraska, and most cross-country hikers that I have spoken with more-or-less stopped cooking by Nebraska or Colorado, too. By that time, most have found their preferred way to get massive calories with the least amount of effort and cost. For most, that means a staple meal (in my case, trail mix) and ENORMOUS meals at restaurants every now and again. By "enormous", I mean like one side of the menu plus a milkshake.

Still, there were times on the trail when I wanted or needed a hot meal for a morale boost or because I was sick to death of trail mix. For hot meals, I carried packaged rice/noodle meals that come in flavors like "garlic butter" and "cheddar broccoli". I always buy the cheapest store brand. No matter the brand, these things don't taste that great and are primarily salt and processed starch. But they are calories that are easy to carry. And, look, if you are trying to walk across the country then you just aren't going to have a five course French meal every night.

I often carried ramen noodles, too. Ramen noodles are a great, super cheap and super light trail food for a hot meal, especially with the addition of tuna. I like ramen noodles. I think they taste good. They make me happy. They ain't health food, but, again, a cross-country hike ain't a restaurant tour or a spa vacation. They are loaded with MSG and other nastiness, but they taste good.

* * *

M.W.C. 4: DO NOT MIX SPAM AND RAMEN NOODLES.

One day out East I was really hungry and wanted to add some sort of meat to my ramen noodles. I stopped at the only market on the trail, and they were out of everything except Spam. I'm not much of a meat eater, anyway, so Spam is...it's a challenging food. That night, I made "Spamen". Spamen tastes sort of like one part sewage to ten parts salt. It is a violation of international law to print the recipe for Spamen. Accordingly, I keep the recipe secret.

* * *

For the days I either did big mileage or planned on a big mileage day, I ate a Vigo Cajun rice and beans dish. Rice and beans are a great trail food, maybe even rivaling trail mix. The Vigo brand offer a ton more calories than the other rice packages or ramen noodles, and I needed that from time to time. Rice and beans is a pretty common staple for cross-country hikers. John and Kait Seyal told me that their go-to staple was rice and lentil pilaf. That's about the same thing.

* * *

I had access to freeze dried dinners made especially for backpackers a couple of times on my Walk. You can find these things at stores like REI. Here is the scoop on these: They are expensive and they taste just about the same as a bag of Vigo rice and beans. By all means, buy these if you have unlimited money. For me, they are not even close to worth the price.

D. Protein/Powdered Milk

Now, I can already hear you saying "but what about protein? You need protein! Protein protein protein!" This country suffers from a bizarre protein fetish. I don't remember this protein craze when I was a kid. I guess it's the result of late nights eating ice cream and flipping between Atkins Diet infomercials and Pumping Iron on the old TiVo. Look, you don't need that much protein and it isn't too hard to get plenty of quality protein.

First of all, there's protein in plants, although no one believes that. Secondly, there's a ton of protein in nuts and seeds. So there's really no reason to worry about a protein deficiency. Still, people are manic about this protein issue, so we Walkers get a lot of questions about this.

From time to time, a Walker can add a can of tuna to a prepared meal. Cans of tuna are really heavy and the can must be carried off the trail to a trashcan, so tuna is hardly worth it when hiking under the pack. Tuna also comes in foil packets, and those are a lot better and lighter. When I added tuna to my meals, it was mostly for taste and as a treat—more of a morale booster than anything.

A Walker who is serious about making miles and keeping pack weight light (and who is not lactose intolerant) should focus on whey powder/powdered milk for protein.

* * *

Powdered milk is the greatest invention in the history of trail food. In my regular life, I don't drink milk at all. But powdered milk is a peerless source of protein and carbs on the trail. It is light, is usually fortified with vitamins A and D, and it is quick and easy to make. Most grocery stores carry powdered milk, usually as a box of powder but often as a box of individually bagged quart servings. If you have never seen it, it looks kind of like white crystals about five or six times the size of a grain of salt. Pour a packet into a quart-sized water bottle, fill with water and shake. Then, boom! Dinner.

So if you are one of those people obsessed with protein, here's your answer. You know when you buy those protein bars and it says "whey protein" in the ingredients? Or those ridiculous tubs of protein powder that *everyone* seems to have in their homes these days? This is where it comes from.

And powdered milk is time-tested, empire approved. Powdered milk products fueled Kublai Khan's Mongol troops as they hiked around conquering one fifth of the world's land. The Mongol empire stretched from the Pacific Ocean to the Black Sea. Those wily Mongols dominated something like a quarter of the Earth. And how did they do it? Powdered milk.

Horses may have helped the Mongols, too. But mostly it was powdered milk. I'm not even making that up—you can look it up. Ok, NEXT ISSUE!

E. Fat

The Walker should carry a fat source on a cross-country walk. Best practice is to carry olive oil. Fat is an essential part of any diet. Judging by the looks of me, it may be a little *too* essential. And, I can tell you from experience that trying to hike 20 miles every day without any fat intake ain't fun at all. And if it ain't fun, then what is the point?

Accordingly, I added fat every time I prepared a meal on the trail and tried to make sure I ate some fat every time I ate. Trail mix comes ready-made with plenty of healthy fats in the nuts and seeds, but any nasty packaged and prepared dinners like I wrote about a second ago call for added fat.

I carried ghee with me when I started the walk. Ghee is clarified butter, a super high calorie fat that keeps quite a while without refrigeration. It is kind of hard to find in most grocery stores I visit, so I made my own. Making ghee is a test of patience, though, and, like an idiot, I stored it in glass bottles. Glass is heavy. I gave up on ghee fairly quickly in favor of olive oil.

Olive oil is easy to find, it comes in light plastic bottles, and it doesn't require refrigeration. Plus, it tastes great. I added olive oil to all of the prepared food I made in camp. John Seyal once confessed to me that one of his favorite meals on the walk was to open a brick of ramen noodles, slather them in olive oil, and eat them without cooking them.

F. Energy Bars, Protein Bars, and Emergency Food

The Walker should not rely on "energy bars", "protein bars", or "meal replacement bars". People tend to think that energy bars are in the same class of food as trail mix. I don't think so. For me, trail mix is a daily food, suitable for snacking and for whole meals, but I consider most bars to be "emergency food". I meet a lot of day hikers who carry PowerBars and Cliff Bars and the like with them. For me, that just seems expensive and unnecessary.

* * *

Walkers will from time to time need to consume sugar, like immediately. If a Walker is not careful and walks too far without eating, then the muscles begin screaming for sugar. In my opinion, there isn't anything better than a Snickers in these situations. For me (and many other hikers I've talked to), a Snickers is the cheapest way to get 2 or 3 hours worth of quick energy. Snickers bars are nasty, processed sugar demons, but they work. It would be nice to always have access to fresh fruit, but it just isn't always possible.

I've talked to a ton of hikers who agree with me on this.

The humble Snickers bar has one drawback, though: They melt. Melted Snickers on a hot day work just the same, but eating them is not very aesthetically pleasing.

So, no, I did not rely on PowerBars or MetRx protein bars, or any other "meal replacement" bars, because trail mix and Snickers do the job a lot cheaper. I'm sure that there are meal replacement bars out there that are great products, but I haven't found them.

* * *

Protein bars taste especially awful and require about two liters of water with each one or else you will suffer some serious gastrointestinal consequences. And who knows where they get the "protein"? They often say it is whey protein and, if it is, then why not just rely on powdered milk a lot cheaper? Sometimes, when they add protein to items, like bagels for example, I have heard they synthesize the protein from human hair collected at Hindu temples in India. I don't know if that is true, but it is freaky enough to scare me away.

G. Sports Drinks and Salt

Walkers should carry a salt supplement to maintain electrolyte levels (at least in the hottest weather). The most common method of electrolyte replacement is drinking sports drinks, but there are also salt tablets and supplements available.

* * *

One craving that most cross-country hikers experience is the craving for salt. In addition to causing a strong (and strange) craving, salt deficiency can cause cramping and a host of other problems.

Humans perspire to keep cool while hiking through hot weather, and the perspiration costs the body both water and electrolytes. There are quite a few electrolytes, including potassium and magnesium. But chief among electrolytes is sodium—the humble salt. We die without salt because the body uses salt to regulate fluid levels on the cellular level.

When the body is low on sodium and chloride—think *table salt*—it causes a condition called *hyponatremia*. Hyponatremia is a very dangerous condition because a) it could kill you, and b) the symptoms look a lot like dehydration, but if treated with more water it gets worse. Hyponatremia, like dehydration, can lead to muscle cramping, fatigue, confusion, etc. It's ugly. And anyone who has worked (or hiked) long hours in the hot, hot Sun knows that it is important to replace salts in the body. The medical jury is out on whether electrolyte replacement drinks are worthwhile—the medical literature indicates that they are not. The medical journals that I looked at say that the single most important factor in exercise induced hyponatremia is *over*-hydration...drinking so much that you weight *more* at the end of the day than when you started. Now, in the old days, farmers and runners and football players used salt tablets to replenish the body's electrolyte stores.

113

Plain old salt tablets are great, but sodium and chloride are only two of the electrolytes that the body needs. Thankfully, well-meaning corporations have come to save us! In today's crazy hectic world, the most common way to replace electrolytes is by drinking massive amounts of sweetened sports drinks like Gatorade. People do this all the time despite the fact that they live sedentary lives and probably have a God's plenty of salt and magnesium and everything else coursing around in their bodies. The mind boggles at this, but there it is.

On a cross-country hike, a cold and fruity sports drink after a long hike is not always a great thing. Sometimes they taste great, but sometimes they are far too sweet and cold for drinking in the hot weather and can cause queasiness. Plus, these drinks are expensive and there are cheaper alternatives.

When I walked across America, a very kind long-distance bicyclist turned me on to a product called Nuun. Nuun, and many other companies, make sugar-free electrolyte replacement tabs that dissolve in water. Nothing tastes better if you are thirsty and need salts. They are much cheaper than sports drinks and weigh very little. For these reasons, I prefer electrolyte replacement tablets to expensive and sugary sports drinks.

* * *

In addition to salt supplements like Nuun tablets, the Walker should also try to eat electrolyte rich foods. For example, green leafy vegetables are high in potassium. (Everyone thinks that bananas are high in potassium, but they aren't particularly—although they are easily digested and are a fairly cheap, high calorie food.) Salted nuts and snacks often have sodium, chloride, and magnesium.

The important message here is that the Walker should understand that he or she needs salt as well as water.

H. Everything Else That Gets All Ate Up

The average Walker eats a lot of just about every kind of food on a cross-country hike. Here are a few trail foods and food tips that some people swear by:

1. Pop tarts. Quick and easy; most Walkers eat so many that they get sick of them. Put peanut butter on them.
2. Bagels. Great source of calories, won't get smashed like regular bread, but kind of bulky and a short shelf life. Put peanut butter on them.
3. Peanut butter. Wonderful; put peanut butter on it.
4. Fresh vegetables. They don't travel well, so eat a lot of fresh fruit and veggies when you are in town and resting. (If you have car support, it's easy to carry fresh vegetables with you.) Put peanut butter on them.
5. Gas station fruit pies. Delicious; don't be afraid to put peanut butter on them.
6. Soda pop. Soda pop is an awful invention; the only people who should be allowed to drink it are cross-country hikers. The best kinds are orange, grape, and Mexican Coca-Cola.
7. Cans of beans. Excellent and amazing; the most honest trail food.
8. Donuts. Horrible invention; eat them liberally. Put peanut butter on them.
9. Milk shakes. Everyone wants to have a milk shake every day. When you walk across the United States, you can.

I. Guilty Pleasures

Most of the dietary "rules" that people live by in regular life do not apply on a cross-country hike. The Walker shouldn't sweat it over guilty pleasures, for example. In real life, a lot of guilty pleasures are bad for you and may make you feel bad about yourself, or whatever. But on the road, it's fine.

My guilty pleasure on the walk was probably either grape soda or gas station fruit pies with peanut butter on them, two things that I never consume in real life. Nate Damm's guilty pleasure was energy drinks, he says. He even says that he guesses that a whole **one quarter of his budget** went to soda/energy drinks. He drank two 16 oz cans of energy drinks a day while he walked across America. That's a lot. *I* would advise you against that, but what do I know, right? Right.

> "It's ok to have stupid, guilty pleasures on the road. I drank energy drinks like a mofo…. They were heavy, horrendously expensive, and very bad for me, but f*** it! I sleep on the ground, never shower, and almost get hit by cars every day. I deserve it!"
> --Nate Damm

Wise words, right there. Damm wise words.

S

   L

      E

        E

          E

            E

              E

                P

VII. WHERE TO SLEEP

Independently wealthy folks can ignore this section. The wealthy Walker (if there is such a thing) can just stay in great motels all the way across the country and never be uncomfortable. As for the rest of us—it's a bitter irony that sleep, which is about the most boring thing in the world, is potentially the most expensive part of a Walk. This is where the Walker should cut corners as much as possible: camp, camp, camp.

There are generally four types of sleeping arrangements for the cross-country hiker. They are: 1) Campgrounds and RV parks, 2) motels, 3) yard camping and staying with friends, and 4) stealth camping.

A. Campgrounds and RV Parks

Most nights on a Walk are spent in a tent. The best places to camp are those where it is legal to camp, so we'll start with campgrounds and RV parks.

A(1) RV Parks

Many RV parks offer camping for a fee. On my trip, I ran into a few RV parks that didn't offer tent camping *until I asked*, and then they agreed—but since they didn't generally offer it, they charged me no fee. There are nice folks in the world.

The best way to find RV parks is a Google search or a search on Google Maps. It's best practice to call ahead and make sure that the park allows tent camping and that the park is actually still open. The fee for tent camping at an RV park is usually between $10 and $20, often closer to $10, so it's cheaper than many standard campgrounds. Many RV parks don't technically offer tent camping because no one has ever asked them. No one has ever asked them because very few people are idiotic enough to try to hike across America. Even these parks that don't technically offer tent camping will sometimes allow tent camping for a nominal fee so long as the camper is kind and appreciative.

M.W.C. 2: DON'T BE AN ASSHOLE.

If you're a professional—an attorney, for example—then there is a pretty high chance that you spend most of your time acting like an asshole, whether you realize it or not. Don't be ashamed or sad about that—it gets better. Spend a few weeks on the road and you'll feel a great deal better about yourself and other people and you'll begin interacting with other primates normally again.

A(2) Campgrounds, State and National Parks

There are campgrounds all across the nation. There are often established campgrounds in national parks, state parks, state forests, and national forests. Some cities allow camping in their municipal parks, some don't. Some are nicer than others.

Campgrounds run in price from $0/night, in the case of national or state forests, to $30/night, $40/night, or even $50/night in the case of some for-profit national chains of campgrounds, which shall remain nameless.

If there is a fee for camping, the campground should offer a bathroom or outhouse, an electrical outlet, and water. Many fee campgrounds will also have soda vending machines. When a cross-country hiker finds a fee campground that does not offer these basic services, then sometimes that cross-country hiker feels justified in sneaking in after dark, camping in secret, and then leaving before sunrise without paying because the campground is a rip-off.

* * *

A Walker will camp in a few national and state parks. These are amazing resources, and should be respected. Walkers should always pay the fee to camp in these parks because they are public treasures. If a Walker arrives after close, there is usually after-hours sign-in. Park rangers usually come by around 10 p.m. or so and collect. Or, the Walker can pay in the morning. But *always* pay the fees in national and state parks.

One thing to remember is that camping areas in state and national parks are always absolutely as far away from the gate as possible and atop the highest point in the park. These parks are designed for cars, not people, and that's a great shame. Walkers should budget anywhere from 2 to 5 extra miles at the end of a day to reach camping areas in national and state parks.

A(3) Municipal Parks

Many towns have some sort of municipal park. I was surprised to find that some municipal parks actually have a policy of allowing camping, usually for a very small fee. Many, however, do not allow camping. But I would say that *most* small Midwestern towns don't have a policy one way or another on whether camping is allowed in their parks. Town officials often sound surprised when asked. If there were more of us walking across America, then I bet they would all adopt a policy of allowing camping for a small fee.

IDEA
Maybe the federal government should sponsor a "walk across America" program? That's a great idea. I'm going to write my congressman. You should, too! Let's call it Wayfare America, or the

"Annual Walk Across America For Mabel", or AWAAFM. Golden idea, right there.

If you play your cards right, you can stay in municipal parks and save a ton of cash. Here is cross-country hiker Nate Damm's take on municipal parks:

"[If] you know what town you're going end your day in, call the local police dispatch, either a local police department or county sheriff dispatch. Having a smart phone comes in really handy here so you can Google this information. If you don't have a smart phone, just ask someone where the police station is and show up there in person. That works too.

So, you call them. They answer. *Say exactly this*:

'*Hey (Operator's Name if they say it), just have a quick question for you. My name is (your name) and I'm walking across America. I'm planning on finishing my day of walking today in (town name) and was wondering if there is anywhere that I might be able to set up my tent and get some sleep for the night, like a town park or a place like that?*'

This works almost every time, and I did it very often. The police are your friends. Be courteous and personable and they'll help you out.

If for some reason they do not help you, do not be rude. Be just as nice as if they had helped you. I say this because one time a police dispatcher said there was nowhere I could camp and that she couldn't help me. I kindly thanked her for her time and told her to have a nice night. Five minutes later she called me back, said that she felt bad and had made a few extra calls, and I was all set to camp in a place outside of town. It pays to be nice, always."

--Nate Damm

Mr. Damm originally shared that piece of information at www.natedamm.com. I asked his permission to share it with you here, and he granted me permission to share it. Why? Because cross-country hikers stick together, Friend. We are tight.

A(4) Bureau of Land Management Camping

I almost didn't include this section, because it's such a nice surprise to discover on your own. But here we go!

The Bureau of Land Management (BLM) manages a tremendous amount of land in the West. Most is public use land, which means that you (as a member of the public) can use it. There are very few rules or regulations on BLM land. Basically, you cannot murder, rape, deal drugs, or commit treason. But just about everything else goes, I think—you can have a fire, let your dogs off the leash, and fire off your .50 caliber machine gun. And cross-country hikers can camp anywhere on BLM land.

It's a game changer for a cross-country hiker.

Once the cross-country hiker gets out west, the BLM land and national forests present ample opportunity for free, legal camping. Stealth camping becomes a thing of the past and there is very little stress about finding a place to sleep.

Check out the BLM website for maps of BLM land. If a cross-country hiker is strong, dedicated, and lucky enough to make it all the way to Utah, then the world opens up. You can pretty much walk all day and then just pull off the side of the road and camp wherever. It's unreal.

One caution, though: As with everywhere, it's best to hide yourself away a bit when camping at night in the desert, especially if you feel vulnerable and scared. The desert at night can be quite intimidating and there's always a chance that a weirdo might set upon your camp in the middle of the night, kill you, steal your water, and then head off to Mexico with the gold you're carrying. That's doesn't happen very often these days, but I've read enough Western novels to know that it's a danger.

B. Motels

Motels should be avoided as much as possible. There are three types of motels: 1) expensive, 2) regular, and 3) "independent". I have no experience with expensive motels, so you're on your own on that one.

Regular motels include the following, roughly from cheaper to more expensive: Motel 6, Red Roof Inn, Super 8, Days Inn, Comfort Inn. Sometimes you'll run into a surprise Super 8 that is quite nice. Same with Red Roof Inn—some are really nice, for apparently no reason. All of these motels are fine. They run from about $50/night to about $120/night. Here's what the Walker needs to know: Spend as little time in all of them as possible, haggle for a cheaper price, tell them about the cross-country hike and they might cut a deal. Here's a little information that only a seasoned traveler would know: Every Motel 6 across the country is exactly like every other Motel 6 and they are all clean; Super 8s, on the other hand, run the gamut from extremely nice for the price to awful.

M.W.C. 22.5: SUPPORT LOCAL AND INDEPENDENT BUSINESSES AS OFTEN AS POSSIBLE.

The third kind of motel is the "independent" motel. These are the best motels on a Walk because they are the cheapest and you never know what you'll get. Rooms in some indie motels go for as little as $20/night, not even kidding. (Some are even *cash only*.) Some independent motels are fronts for drugs and/or prostitution. Some are quite charming and some are much more awful than you could imagine. There are people who live in some of them for extended periods of time.

The Walker should favor independent motels because they are cheap and because these are where Walkers meet the most interesting people and the scariest people; this is where a lot of great stories take place. If you wonder what kind of "great stories" you might have in indie motels, check out *By Men or By the Earth* for the "Story of Tyler Accidentally Happening Upon a Mexican Masturbation Party in a Small Nebraska Town." Weird experience, right there.

C. Yard Camping

Right-o! This is where the good stuff is. Many people are interested in cross-country hikers and the story that cross-country hikers have to tell—it's something that most people don't have the guts to do, and the few who have the guts likely won't have the opportunity. Some people who hear the story will want to help.

The Walker should talk with people at every chance, should be kind and courteous, and should smile, but not too much. It's best practice not to curse, and the Walker should never take the Lord's name in vain or mention politics. The Walker who sticks to these basic rules will eventually (probably frequently) be invited to sleep on folks' yards.

Begging is not necessary and is not encouraged, but there is nothing wrong with asking for a place to sleep. Walkers should try to make a good impression and try not to give people any reason for fear. The Walker should use caution if approaching houses or knocking on doors. It's necessary from time to time, but a lot of people don't like to be bothered by homeless weirdos asking to camp on their yard.

M.W.C. 41.2: TRY TO MAKE A GOOD IMPRESSION.

Best practice is to develop an "elevator pitch" to request yard camping. It should be a short, friendly, and exciting explanation of the Walk. A pitch like this greatly increases the chances of securing yard camping, especially when the Walker shows humility. Humility and kindness go a long way. Good people respond to good ideas and will often help out with a lawn to crash in.

* * *

Here are the rules for yard camping: Be quiet, be clean; don't disturb the hosts and always clean up; camp only where the hosts say to camp, even if it's on an awful hill and underneath a tree.

M.W.C. 43: IF SOMEONE INVITES YOU TO SLEEP ON THEIR YARD OR IN THEIR HOUSE, EAT WHATEVER THEY OFFER TO YOU.

It's bad manners to turn down hospitality. I, for example, do not eat red meat and haven't for almost 20 years—but if someone had offered me a steak, I would have eaten it because you *do not turn down that kind of hospitality.*

* * *

When yard camping, the two biggest dangers are: 1) scaring people while asking for camping, such that they call the police (which will very rarely happen), and 2) accidentally camping in the yard of a crazy person. The second danger is very real and happens to most Walkers at least once. There's no foolproof, 100% accurate way of predicting where crazy persons live. Nate Damm has a good tip, though:

> "More than one car in the driveway is typically a good sign; two insane people living together is much less likely than one crazy person living alone."
> --Nate Damm

There are other signs that might indicate a crazy person lives there, as well. For example, if there is a sign that begins "By Order of the court..." or "In compliance with state law..." then it might not be the best place to yard camp. Likewise, signs that read "Trespassers will be shot" or "WARNING: THIS IS MY CASTLE AND I STAND MY GROUND" are pretty good indicators to keep them doggies movin' for a few blocks.

D. Stealth Camping

Alright, let's be honest: You're a smart guy or gal, you know how things work, so you can figure out how to call an RV park or find a campground; you've checked into motels before. What you haven't done is stealth camp. You probably don't even know what stealth camping is because you've lived a life of quiet desperation, Man. It's time to break out of your little workaday world, take some chances.

So what is stealth camping? Well, slow down, Captain...let's start with what stealth camping *is not*. Stealth camping *is not* trespassing. Stealth camping *is* setting up a camp and sleeping in a place where the legality of camping there is...less than settled.

Let me make clear that stealth camping is a last resort. A Walker will have days when he or she cannot find a place to sleep for the night. It will happen. In these moments of last resort, stealth camping is the practice that allows a person to enjoy relatively peaceful nights while attracting absolutely the least amount of attention possible.

* * *

Stealth camping is stressful the first few times. It is scary to watch night fall without a place to sleep secured for the night. But eventually it's just a part of life on the road.

The Walker should remember that the world becomes a very different place after dark. Nate Damm advises:

"It doesn't make sense to get upset, frustrated, or scared when you can't find a place to sleep. When it gets dark, you can hide pretty much anywhere there is a shadow, and there are plenty to choose from. Worst-case scenario, you have to get up really early. That's no big deal. There is ALWAYS some place to sleep."

--Nate Damm

D(1) Where to Stealth Camp

People *can* camp wherever the hell they want to. Whether a person *may* or *should* camp in a particular spot is a different matter. When it comes to stealth camping, some places are much better than others.

Groves of trees are a great resource for stealth camping. In the East there are often groves of trees just off the roadside. It's best practice to look for places where the view from the road is obstructed. There are often obscured places in or near forested areas just off the road where one can keep a low profile. Many of these areas sometimes have a "no trespassing" sign posted somewhere. The two possible responses to "no trespassing" signs are to 1) not pay very much attention, so as to avoid seeing those signs, or 2) move along when you see a no trespassing sign far enough that a reasonable person wouldn't think that the sign necessarily applies.

But there are no trees in the Great Plains. Once into the Great Plains, and in some parts of the Midwest, it is very difficult to find tree cover to stealth camp. In areas like this, most stealth camping is done behind disused and abandoned buildings.

In general, the search for a stealth camping spot should focus on areas outside of small towns, rather than inside the towns. (In big cities, it's a whole different world—I've done almost no stealth camping inside big cities.) There are often old churches in the countryside in the Midwest, often right on the cross-country path, and these are sometimes good to camp behind.

* * *

M.W.C. 56: DON'T COUNT ON ANYONE 100%.

A Walker can never count on being welcomed behind a church or on church property. Still, stealth camping on church property is marginally safer than on non-church property for three reasons. One, people pay less attention and don't look behind churches. Two, who owns the church? No one knows! And three, most importantly, the folks who actually run the church are probably decent folks who will listen to you and help you out. Not always! But mostly.

Other great stealth camping locations include, but are not limited to, abandoned buildings, beside (but not in) cornfields when the corn is high, and underneath bridges.

* * *

M.W.C 38.2: DON'T HIDE IN DANGEROUS PLACES.

The Walker should never camp in a developed agricultural plot. As much as possible, the Walker should avoid camping even *near* an agricultural plot. So in general, there is no stealth camping in cornfields or bean fields, etc.

There are two reasons for this: 1) People tend to operate very heavy machinery in corn fields and those machines can run over and kill a person without the driver even seeing the person—trust me on that one, as I grew up in a farming community and on my Grandpa's farm; and 2) Corn fields are someone's livelihood and folk don't take kindly to you trampling around in their livelihood. If stealth camping is a last resort, then camping in or near an agricultural area is the last resort of the last resort. Best practice is to avoid agricultural plots.

D(2) How to Stealth Camp

There are very few hard and fast rules for stealth camping. It is a blood sport. It is the black bloc tactic of the cross-country hiker. When a person is stealth camping, the person is actively rejecting the fundamental convention of Western society: The exclusionary right of private property. Instead, the stealth camper declares him or herself free of all legal conventions that are not based on the harm principle. The trick is to make that declaration very, very quietly.

Here is how one might do it.

First, the process begins early. The need for stealth camping is usually apparent and considered around 3 or 4 p.m. Scouting for a stealth spot begins several hours before sunset. If a Walker finds a good place long before Sunset, it's necessary to decide whether to keep pushing miles for the day or to slow down, hide out, double back and camp.

M.W.C. 44: INFORMATION IS WORTH ITS WEIGHT.

If the Walker has a cell phone with data service, he or she could use satellite images on Google Maps to scout out territory miles in front. It's sometimes possible to identify stealth camping areas far in advance by using this method. However, information gleaned from Google Maps is not always reliable.

* * *

Once all other sleeping options are exhausted, having decided to stealth camp, *and* after locating a good spot, the Walker then becomes sneaky. Best practice is to not enter a stealth camping spot until after dark. A stealth camper should not mill around loitering all day waiting for the Sun to go down, either.

The Walker should enter the stealth camping area quietly under the cover of night and set up camp as quietly as possible. When stealth camping, "setting up your camp" means pitching your tent and nothing more. If possible, it's better to not even set up a tent—just roll out a sleeping bag and get into it. Hard sleepers should make sure to set an alarm to wake them prior to sunrise. One key to successful stealth camping is to wake up before the Sun and to get the hell out of there.

In the morning, the stealth camper must erase every trace of camping. This is where "leave no trace" really, really applies.

* * *

M.W.C. 38: WHEN YOU NEED TO HIDE, BE HIDDEN.

This is common sense but it is important to remain hidden when stealth camping. Therefore, in stealth camping there is:

- No cooking.
- No open flame.
- No music.
- No flashlight.
- No smart phone.

Best practice is to assume that if someone sees a stealth camper then someone will soon be coming to check on the stealth camper.

I was lucky when I walked across America in that I only got busted stealth camping twice. Both were my fault. I was busted once while setting camp before it was dark and a fellow who was awfully scared of me asked me to move along. I moved along. The other time a fellow came upon me while I was hunkered into my tent in the middle of nowhere behind an old building. That second fellow was awfully drunk, which could have been a horrible scene. For some reason that is completely unknown to me, the conversation went like this:

"What the hell are you doin'?"

"Sleeping. I'm walking across the United States with my dog and I ran out of sunlight."

"Ran out of sunlight? Well now I've heard everything. Causin' trouble?"

"Not yet," I said.

"Well, then. Sorry to bother you!"

Sunshine

Lollipops

Rainbows

Everything

VIII. ROUTING AND WEATHER

The only rule of routing that is set in stone is that the route will change in unexpected ways, often when least expected. Some people might decide to hit the trail without any maps or any routing plans at all and just "go where life takes them". I don't recommend that.

As for weather, there is no way to be 100% sure about the weather, but the Walker should try to have a general idea of what is possible and what to expect.

A. Routing Needs

I advise carrying two routing tools, both maps. One, as I mentioned earlier, Google Maps is incredible. Two, paper maps. Paper maps are necessary in areas where there is no cell service and are far more practical to use for routing and research in the West and Southwest. In the West and Southwest, the Walker spends a lot of time reviewing the map, and that's better done on paper. There are two options for paper maps: a big old road atlas like your parents used to have in the trunk of their Buick, or folding state maps that are available at many gas stations. I went with a travel-sized coast-to-coast atlas, and it was essential.

The Walker should know how to read maps. It's not difficult. The Walker should probably also carry a decent quality cheap compass, although it will almost certainly not be needed. Again, remember that a compass is useless if the Walker doesn't know how to use it. It's not very difficult to learn to use a compass. But here's why it's not necessary: A cross-county hike runs east to west, so the Walker wakes up and walks with the Sun at his or her back for about six hours and then walks into the sun for about six hours. Easy.

A(1) Choosing and Adjusting The Route

A workable route must take into consideration access to resources, road construction, impassable roads, and mountains, to name just a few things. I recommend choosing a basic idea of a route, collecting information about the route along the way, and changing the route as necessary to meet needs and to avoid dangers.

To pick a route, look at a map.

> "U.S. Road Atlas all the way, baby; you can walk on anything yellow, black, or red. Pretty easy to use for idiots like myself."
> --Nate Damm

Maps provide a general idea of how far it is between towns and how far one might need to walk to find food or water. But it's vital to collect information along the way, as well, because maps are not always current. People who *actually live there* might have a little better information than a map, especially with regard to mountain passes and road construction. When asking people how far to a grocery store, or how far to Nebraska, best practice is to double and triple check *all* information from locals because they are often wrong. Plus, most folks have never walked long distances. What they perceive as "about two miles" might actually be 25 miles. What they perceive as "oh, Man, at least 15 miles!" might actually be around 400 yards.

* * *

The Google Maps terrain function can help estimate elevation changes in the route. A general rule of thumb is to add an extra hour of travel time for every 1000 feet in elevation change—that's probably an understatement, though. The Google Maps terrain function can help to minimize the amount of climbing in a route. Most of the time it is not possible to completely avoid climbing by re-routing, but it is at least better to know what to expect.

When routing, it is also best to remember that the Google Maps satellite feature can be used to scout potential stealth camping spots ahead as well as potential shady spots. These considerations might impact routing choices, as well.

A(2) How Long Will it Take?

There is no certain answer to this question because far too many variables and individual peculiarities determine hiking speed. Some people are slower than others, and any difficulty in the path will slow down the hike, from weather, to elevation, to the weight of the pack.

Backpacking/hiking literature provides various estimates for average hiking speed. In general, average speed estimates seem to fall between two and three miles per hour on flat ground and that an hour should be added for every 1000 feet in elevation gain.

* * *

My cross-country hike took 8 months. Nate Damm did it in about 7 months, or a little over, but he took a couple weeks off to go to some sort of convention or something. John and Kait Seyal took a little over 8 months, but they were busy the whole way doing therapy dog visits. Dogs and recalcitrant hiking partners both slow hikes tremendously.

If I had to do it again, I'd set a goal of 5 months and I'm pretty certain I would make that. But a first time Walker should probably count on longer than 5 months and should allow at least 9 months.

B. Weather

Of all the things that might kill a Walker, the weather is probably the second most likely. (The most likely is a car and a bad driver.) Remember:

> **M.W.C. 8: THE EARTH WILL KILL YOU IF YOU ARE NOT CAREFUL; IT HAS NO EMOTIONS.**

There are basically four types of weather that could kill a hiker. They are: 1) cold and rainy weather, 2) hot weather, 3) lightning, and 4) wind. Let's take them in order.

Cold and rainy weather is probably the most dangerous. It is possible to stay dry in cold weather and even in snow. And if you can stay dry, you can probably stay warm. But when it is cold and rainy you will have a bad time. Equipment and clothes get soaked, and that's bad all around. My way of dealing with cold and rainy weather was to set rules of engagement. If the weather was below forty-five degrees and raining, we did not walk. If the weather was below forty degrees and rain was in the forecast, we did not walk. I set these strict rules of engagement because I felt that was the point at which it was unsafe for my dog, Mabel. In truth, those are pretty cold temperatures in the rain for humans, too. But in my experience, it was important to set those rules of engagements ahead of time so that they took away any question of whether to walk or not—if it's too cold, the rules of engagement kick in and we stayed put, stayed warm, and didn't die.

When it comes to cold weather, know your clothing and know your limitations. Don't die of hypothermia.

* * *

Hot weather is just as dangerous. Walkers with dogs should remember that the hot weather is far *more* dangerous for dogs because humans are so much better adapted to hot weather. We can take off layers, put on hats and carry umbrellas to stay out of the Sun. Most people can keep walking in pretty extreme heat with enough water and a wide-brimmed hat. But for dogs—or at least for my dog—it becomes unsafe around 85 degrees. At 80 degrees we had to start slowing; at 85, we went very slowly, stopping frequently. At 87 degrees, we stopped. Full stop. No questions. We just stopped.

At 87 degrees, I felt it was too hot for Mabel, so we found shade and stopped. I love Mabel and I didn't want to put her in danger.

When it comes to hot weather, know your limitations. Don't die of hyperthermia or dehydration.

* * *

Lightning is a danger in the higher elevations of the West, especially when crossing mountain passes. When on top of a mountain pass, a Walker is much higher than most everything around, which makes the Walker an attractive target for lightning. Know this. One time in Colorado, I timed my hike so poorly that I was on the exact highest point of a mountain pass during a violent lightning storm. Lightning crashed all around. We had to run downhill in the rain with a big pushcart in front of us on a road with a small shoulder. It was a very bad time.

When there is lightning, the wise Walker gets low and doesn't get struck by lightning.

* * *

Finally, wind. Wind can be dangerous but it's usually nothing to worry about. I'll deal with this danger in the widow maker section of the "Selecting a Campsite" section of this book.

B(1) Weather Resources

Predicting the weather is another advantage of carrying a smart phone because the walker has only two options for checking forecasts: a phone and asking people.

The Walker should Google the weather and Google it often. It changes a lot and weather forecasters are usually 83% inaccurate, 62% of the time.

The Walker should be especially careful of the weather in Illinois, Iowa, and the Great Plains. The timing of a cross-country hike puts the Walker out there during summer when nasty thunderstorms can grow, sweep over you, and blow the hell out of you before you realize it.

THIS MOMENT IS YOUR LIFE

(AND SO IS THIS ONE)

(AND THIS ONE)

(AND THIS ONE)

(AND THIS...)

IX. All the People

All cross-country hikers meet a great many people. Some people are interested in learning about hikers, and some people are interested in hassling hikers. Some people are cops and some people are preachers. Some people just want to hand someone a five-dollar bill or a sandwich. Cross-country hikers meet *all* the people.

When I walked across America I saw the best and the worst of people. They never stopped surprising me with how generous they can be, or with how horrible they can be. Cross-country hikers have a tendency to view their hike through rose-colored glasses, or at least to describe it through rose-colored glasses. So when a hiker says, "Oh, you'll meet the best people and the experience will re-affirm your faith in mankind!", that hiker is not *lying*, but isn't telling the whole truth, either.

All that said, most of this section should be Common Sense. Perhaps review it, but you should know all of this.

A. Trail Magic

Trail magic is a stupid term, because there's nothing magic about it and there's no such thing as magic. John, Kait, Nate—they might believe in "trail magic", but I haven't asked them about the term. I've come to realize for myself that "trail magic" is really just "common human decency" pushed to a little bit of an extreme. But, Man, it makes a trip like this sing. It's a beautiful thing done by beautiful people.

It happens when someone who you do not know offers you great comfort at no benefit to him or herself. Sometimes it's food; sometimes it's a place to sleep. Sometimes it's a pair of clean, new socks and sometimes it's just great conversation.

If a Walker's prime motivation is to experience trail magic, then the Appalachian Trail is the best place for it. It's rampant over there. There are even places where people pitch big old tents with tons of food in them and just wait for hikers to come by. Some people put coolers full of food out by the trail and just leave it there. It's ridiculous.

On the American Discovery Trail? It will happen, but don't expect it. And on a Walk it *will* happen, but it can never be counted on.

A(1) How to Accept Trail Magic

Be cordial and respectful, and *always* say thank you. Sometimes it's nice to say thank you a couple of times.

A Walker shouldn't cry when receiving trail magic. That sounds like silly advice, but here's the deal: At some point, a Walker will need something desperately and someone will, for no reason at all, show up and provide it. The resulting feeling will be close to overwhelming. But a Walker shouldn't cry, because that will make the "trail angel" feel nervous, self-aware

* * *

Walkers meet people who live near established trails who *regularly* host hikers. Into their homes! I stayed with families in Delaware, West Virginia, Ohio, and Iowa.

In Maryland, a woman left a bag of food for me and a bag of food for Mabel alongside the road.

In the heat in Nebraska, a couple doubled back 15 miles out of their way to bring cold drinks to Mabel and me.

People gave me food in almost every state, including home cooked meals delivered by strangers alongside the highway in both West Virginia and Utah.

An attorney in New York *sent me an iPad* so that I could write a blog and keep him updated. And an attorney in Delaware sent me a camera because, she said, my "pictures weren't good enough".

It will happen.

* * *

Here's a great tip from the Seyals: Keep a backward guest book. All cross-country hikers (try to) do this, probably, and it's a great thing to do. Everyone should--

"You will meet people and make friends and you'll want to send thank you cards, emails, letters, or photos from the road. You may even want to go back and visit them some day. Carry a pocket-sized address book and treasure it. It will be one of your most precious artifacts from your journey."

--Kait Seyal

A(2) Be Cautious, Be Safe

There are crazies out there, sure. But Walkers don't usually run into many of them. There are bad neighborhoods, too, but Walkers usually walk through them in broad daylight. Still...there is always the potential for a bad encounter with a North American primate.

Be cautious to stay safe and trust your instincts with people. If you get the feeling that this or that person might not be "all there", or might be...you know, crazy...then trust that feeling. It's better to be safe than sorry in these cases.

* * *

When I walked across America, I was alone except for Mabel. For some reason—perhaps my gallant good looks—I did not get much flack from people. I view this as a trade-off: Nate Damm, who is a much better looking young man than I am, got a little bit more flack from people and a great deal more good-natured assistance; I, on the other hand, look a bit like if you hit Henry Rollins in the face with a sledgehammer, dragged his body through the dirt, then put him in prison for three years—as a result, I didn't get much flack from troublesome types and also not nearly as much good-natured assistance.

Probably the biggest people danger out there (except for bad drivers) is groups of teenage boys. Even if you look like an early 1980s punk rocker fresh out of prison, packs of teenage boys might harass you from time to time. That's a bit scary because, as we all know, teenage boys sometimes kill homeless people for fun.

I can't tell someone how to avoid those situations, or really how to handle them. I tried very hard to be kind and considerate to everyone I met on my Walk, and I think I succeeded at that. But from time to time, I had to be a little mean to teenagers. They'll get over it.

Be strong out there.

A(3) The Five-O

Run-ins with the police are almost certain on a cross-country hike. Almost certain. Most cross-country hikers have various horror stories about being escorted out of town, or of being given a place to camp on a police station lawn. Like all people, a cop's reaction to you is largely based on how you treat them. In my experience, you don't have to be a groveling idiot, but you also shouldn't be an asshole.

Kait Seyal says:

> "They will stop and talk to you. They will check you out and want to know what you're up to. They will ask you if you're ok and if you have a baby in your pushcart. Police officers are your friends as long as you are playing by the rules."
>
> --Kait Seyal

I more or less agree. But if smart about it, a person can avoid more run-ins with police than Kait lets on, I think. When I walked across America, I had very few run-ins with police. The one out-and-out bad experience I had was with an off-duty cop in West Virginia who told me to leave his town—which I did not actually do straight away, because he was in the wrong, and I never went to jail. So there's that. Most of my experiences with cops (which I don't count as "run ins") were in the parking lots of gas stations and they went like this:

Cop closes his door and walks toward the door of the gas station; I'm sitting in the shade.

COP: How are you today?

ME: Pretty well, I guess. All things considered. You?

COP: Same old same old.

ME: Cool.

COP: You alright?

ME: Yup. Walking across America.

COP: Really? Why?

ME: Good question.

Then there was some laughter. The cop got his coffee or whatever and we both went on our ways.

Of course the Walker can *probably* assume that he or she will have an encounter with a stereotypically stupid, chip on the shoulder, idiotic police officer. I hate to say that, but it's the truth—there are a few of those types out there. But the overwhelming majority of interactions with the police will likely be positive. Cops, just like people, are usually good folks.

* * *

The Walker should do all they can to put law enforcement at ease, and should not be afraid to use law enforcement as a resource. The police are there to serve and to protect, after all. The Walker should check in with local police if unexpectedly stuck in a town or sleeping in a municipal park. Sometimes friendly police will even allow Walkers to camp on the police station lawn, if the Walker is nice about it.

When police approach, the Walker should be calm and cool. Hands should be visible, on the cart or at least not stuffed into pockets. Smiles go a long way, and it's never good to act twitchy or nervous. Be mindful that cross-country hikers look a bit suspicious and, frankly, badass. Cops don't like to approach suspicious looking badasses—they worry about their own safety, just like everyone else. Don't make quick movement, show ID if asked, be kind and don't be an ass, and 90% of interactions will go well.

A(4) Be Cautious, Be Safe

The Walker should always trust his or her instincts. If, at any time, the Walker feels ill at ease, distrustful, or wary of someone, the Walker should be careful and should leave the situation.

What can you do?
WHAT CAN YOU DO?
WHAT CAN YOU DO!
WHAT CAN YOU DO?

WHAT CAN YOU DO?

X. Skills

A. Selecting a Campsite

Walkers become expert at campsite selection. There are a few rules or suggestions that hold true for selecting campsites in all cases, whether in a park or when stealth camping. When stealth camping, obviously, Walkers have to be more "flexible" with these requirements.

Often, there is limited choice in campsite location, either because of stealth camping or camping in a park with designated spots. But a few considerations are true even in these circumstances.

A(1) Widowmakers

This is vital: Never pitch a tent beneath dead or weak tree limbs. This is so important that it qualified for the Model Rules of Walking:

M.W.C. 8.2: Always check for widow makers before pitching a tent.

A widow maker is a tree limb that falls from the sky in the middle of the night onto a tent and kills all who are sleeping peacefully inside. This is something that actually happens, so Walkers must be careful in selecting a campsite. Most designated camping areas are pretty clear of this kind of thing, but it never hurts to check.

Walkers should take a second to scan the sky before selecting a place to put a tent. Where possible, tents should be pitched beneath a clear, unobstructed view of the sky. If there is *any indication* of something up there that might fall, then don't tent there. In wooded areas, look for tree limbs without leaves on them or with cracks in them because they will be weaker, more likely to fall. Listen for creaking limbs. It's best, of course, to just not tent beneath a tree.

When stealth camping, Walkers sometimes have to make educated guesses about the structural integrity of buildings, bridges, etc. When in doubt when stealth camping, tents should be in shadows rather than beneath things casting shadows.

A(2) Do It Have to Be Grassy? Do it?

Soft, grassy pastures are best for camping. Grass holds the dirt together, so there is less chance of tracking mud into the tent, and it's soft and wonderful to lie upon. Note that ticks like to live in grass. More often than not, though, the Walker has to settle for less-than-ideal conditions.

In all cases, the Walker should look for best possible conditions for tenting at night. If possible, ground should be soft enough (but not muddy) to drive tent stakes into the ground. (Where that is not possible, Walkers can guy out tents on trees, fence posts, large stones or even cars.) Ground should ideally be grassy, or at least bare dirt, and not gravel or rock-bed.

M.W.C.: GO AN EXTRA MILE WHEN IT MATTERS.

It's usually not *necessary* to guy out a freestanding tent, but it's still best practice to do so. It does not take a long time, it's a skill that gets better with practice, and a home should be secure, even if it's a tent.

A(3) Drainage

The tent should ideally be pitched on a very slight slope. It should not be steep or pronounced, but a gradual slope provides a bit of drainage in case of rain and running water. This is especially important when camping near a river or in a lowland area. If there is a sudden downpour in the night, any water rushing beside the tent might wake the camper before the water gathers into a pool, then into a flood, then turns into a thrashing torrent of water that will carry campers away to the sea.

Best practice is to sleep with the head higher on the slope and feet lower.

A(4) Other Considerations

There may be other considerations, too. For example, sick or ill Walkers may want to locate relatively closer to water or restroom facilities. If in need of an electrical outlet, Walkers may want to locate closer to that resource. And, of course, Walkers may have to adjust their campsite to avoid sleeping underneath streetlights.

A(5) Prepare The Space

Once a safe campsite is selected, a Walker should prepare the site to receive a tent. This saves time and money in the form of spared expense fixing punctured tents, and it makes nights more restful.

Use feet, hands, or even a piece of brush or leafy tree branch to sweep the area where the tent will sit. Inspect the area and remove any sticks, stones, or material that might puncture a tent.

Many people skimp on this step. They are too tired or impatient, and they pitch their tent without clearing a bed for it. Skimping this step will usually not result in a puncture, but it only takes one rock or stick to put a hole in a tent that might grow into a rip and then before too long the tent is ruined. Tent fixes are difficult and time consuming, and tent replacement is expensive. So do the right thing: Prepare the site to receive the tent.

B. Starting a Fire

I get it: You're an office-bound na'er do well who can't do manly man things like start a fire. But you're embarrassed to admit that to your friends and colleagues for fear that they'll think you're some sort of a...oh, for shame! I won't even type it.

Look: starting a fire is easy. I'll teach you how.

First, you'll need a tool to start the fire, either a lighter or a magnesium striker, or even matches. (You can also use a couple of piece of wood, but save that for your Bear Grylls fantasies. Out on the trail, use a lighter and be macho about it, Tough Guy.) In addition, you'll need tinder, kindling, and fuel.

Tinder is small, highly flammable material. It burns fast and is easy to light. Think of dryer lint, dry grass, or paper. Kindling is slightly bigger stuff that will burn longer, like twigs. Fuel is, you know, big sticks and logs. Got it? Ok.

M.W.C.: CARRY A BAG OF DRYER LINT AND A TUB OF VASELINE.

Dryer lint is decent tinder as it is, but you cover that stuff in Vaseline and you've got yourself quite a fire-starting resource. Vaseline comes in handy in a number of other instances, too, ranging from securing and waterproofing nuts and bolts to easing chafing on various parts of the body.

* * *

First, collect a bunch of twigs and sticks for kindling and some bigger branches/logs. As a good rule of thumb, gather about twice as much kindling as you think you'll need because it never lasts as long as you think it will and you never have enough. Arrange the kindling in neat stacks sorted by size.

Next, secure your fire pit. If you don't have a fire ring, make one out of stones. If you don't have stones, consider digging a small pit to put your fire in.

Now take some of the small twigs and build a very small house. Remember Lincoln Logs? Did you play with those as a kid? Cool…build a house like that. Put tinder in the middle and maybe a little bit of the kindling. Light the tinder. When it starts to burn or smolder, blow on it. Now feed it until the kindling gets going. Once the kindling gets going, feed it larger kindling, and larger, and larger, and then small logs and then big logs, and larger logs, and larger, and then a tree, and then a forest, and then eventually the whole planet is on fire and you're warm and toasty.

M.W.C.: IF YOU DON'T KNOW HOW TO BUILD AND MAINTAIN A FIRE, FIND SOMEONE TO TEACH YOU.

Walkers need to learn fire safety and etiquette. Try to keep all fires in confined fire rings, where available. If fire rings are not available, dig out a shallow spot and circle it with rocks. You don't want your fire to escape and kill us all. Which could happen. One time Johnny Cash burnt down a whole forest when he tossed out a cigarette. No kidding. That happened.

B(I) Fire Safety Tips

Fire safety is important. I don't want to sound like a stodgy old man, but fire needs to be respected. A lot of people who attempt cross-country hikes are Midwesterners like me or (gasp!) East Coasters, and don't have a real appreciation for how easily a fire can get out of control in the arid West. So some fire safety tips might fall under Common Sense, but it's best to review them, anyway.

- Check for burn bans and respect them; do not start a fire if a burn ban is in place. Burn bans are there for a reason and wildfires are dangerous business.
- Build fires only in designated areas, if there are such areas.
- Secure fires with a stone ring or pit wherever possible.
- Do not sleep next to a fire.
- Make sure your fire has burned down before getting in your tent at night.
- Make sure your tent is a safe distance away from the fire, so that it doesn't catch a spark and burn.
- Extinguish all fires completely before leaving a campsite.

- Do not light a fire if stealth camping.

This list is not exhaustive, but it's a good start for understanding how to fear and respect fire.

C. Shitting

Let's be adults here for a second. You are a lawyer, a doctor, an accountant. You're a professional. You are highly civilized and your life is all put together and awesome. Well, guess what: If you hike across the country, you have to shit in strange places.

That's just how we roll.

I thought long and hard about what to title this section. But here's something that happens to you when you walk across America: You get very serious about basic things, like shitting. And once you get serious, you pick the best words for things. Some people might be offended by the word "shit", but it's the most accurate word. For a fascinating discussion on this, see the book *The Big Necessity*. That book will change the way you think about water and public sanitation. Great book. Ok! Back to work here!

* * *

Here is a list of some of the places that Walkers shit when walking across America: fast food joints, motels, friends' houses, strangers' houses, gas stations, outhouses in parks, port o potties, far away from highways, very close to highways, under bridges, beside trees, in open fields of tall grass, in open fields of no grass, in the sand, on stone, and everywhere else.

Seriously—this is a serious matter, and I think it's one that scares a lot of people who would otherwise do a hike like this. Walkers burn a lot of calories and eat a lot of food, and that creates a lot of waste. That's not a big deal when you're around restrooms. But what about when you're not? There's really not a great deal of literature available on this topic. There is a book called *How to Shit in the Woods*. I've not read it, but people tell me that it's good. I'm betting that the book goes into a bit more detail than you need.

Well, thank me. Here's all you need to know.

First, find a spot. If shy, hide behind a tree or building. If not shy, then squat wherever you feel the need. Keep in mind that defecating in public is likely illegal. I haven't looked that up, but I bet it is.

Don't shit by a stream or by standing water.

After you've found a spot, dig a little hole. It's called a "cat hole". The hole should be a few inches deep—too deep and the waste won't decompose, too shallow and animals and politicians will dig it up. Outdoorsy store clerks will try to sell you a thing called a "trench shovel" or something like that. It's a tiny little garden spade. If you insist on carrying a special small shitting spade, go to a hardware store and get a very cheap garden spade. If you're a rational human being, on the other hand, know that you can dig a hole with your heel, a stick, or a rock.

Undo your trousers and what not and then squat over the hole. Keep in mind that your pants, if they are around your ankles, might potentially be located in a direct line beneath you. You must correct for this by pulling your pants out in front of you or by leaning backward a bit while squatting. The latter method is possible really only with the help of something stable to hold on to and lean against. If you neglect to do either of those steps, you will shit in your pants.

M.W.C. 1: DON'T SHIT IN YOUR PANTS.

Ok, I think you can take it from there. Do your business and then clean yourself up. Then congratulate yourself and cover up the hole. You've just accomplished something that everyone in the history of the world has done.

D. Walking Beside A Highway

149

This is by far the most dangerous thing about walking across America. Walkers *will* nearly be killed. In fact, near death experiences happen almost every day. The trick is to remain *nearly* killed and never *actually* killed.

[*Editor's Note:* I do not want to put too fine a point on it, but I am compelled to mention that I find it hard to believe that no one has yet died on a cross-country hike…or, at least, no one that I have heard of. If enough people attempt such a hike, it will happen.]

One can walk beside almost all county and state highways. One can even walk on the big open shoulders of many limited-access highways. But, as a general rule, it is illegal to walk alongside interstates. That's just as well, because it's dangerous as hell. I spent about 7 miles on an interstate in Utah, but that was because there are only 6 roads in all of Utah so sometimes you have to walk on the interstate out there.

* * *

M.W.C. 16: WALK AGAINST TRAFFIC.

Walkers should amble along on the left side of the road, against traffic. It is infinitely safer and it is the law.

The *only* exception to this is that sometimes, usually when descending from mountain passes, there might be stretches where there is no shoulder on the left and a blind corner on the right. In these rare circumstances it is *sometimes* a decent idea to cross over to the right side. But even in these cases, it's not safe.

In the rare cases where Walkers might switch to the right, it's necessary to cross to the right side far in advance of the blind corner. While proceeding through the corner, Walkers must be very careful and always keep an eye out behind. If rounding a blind corner on the right, Walkers must then *haul ass* on the other side of the corner. This is because cars will come screaming around the corner very close to the right hand shoulder.

* * *

When taking breaks beside the road, the Walker and *all* equipment should be as far off of the road as possible. When walking, the body and all equipment should be off the road as well. Keep it all to the left of the white line. The Walker must **remain vigilant** even while sitting alongside the highway, because cars sometimes veer off the road.

* * *

There are places in the West and Southwest where there is almost no traffic whatsoever. Out there, a man can walk in the middle of the damn road if he wants to. Out there, there are days where a man won't see a car at all. Those are good days. Those are days a man can enjoy.

E. Knots

M.W.C. 55: EVERYONE SHOULD KNOW HOW TO TIE FIVE GOOD KNOTS.

I am mathematics hobbiest and so I'm also a knot aficionado. I learned quite a few knots before I walked across America, and I was certain that my arsenal of awesome knots would come in handy. I found that I didn't use many knots, and most that I had learned were of no use. Still, the Walker needs to know a few different knots for different tasks.

There are several knots that will work for almost every task. But I've identified here the six knots that I used most frequently. Now, I'm not going to explain to you how to make these knots, because that would be difficult for me to write and even harder for you to understand. Instead, I'm going to tell you six knots that I used, then you can go learn them on the Old YouTubeCom.

1. Alpine Butterfly Knot. For hanging equipment in your tent or on your belt, or adding handles to items.
2. Clove Hitch. For hanging the bear bag. Also, an easy variation makes this a slippery hitch, which is useful for hitching other things.
3. Bow Knot. The bowknot is a slipped reef knot, like you tie on your shoes and it is the most useful knot, probably. Use the bow to tie bundles of anything, like your tarp or your clothes bag, or whatever. Note the difference between a reef knot and a granny knot, and learn to tie the reef knot rather than the granny knot.
4. Bowline hitch. This is a great knot for affixing one end of rope or cord to…well, to anything.
5. Trucker's Hitch, or Power Cinch Knot. This is a useful knot for running guy lines out from your tarp or tent, or for tying down any loads that require adjusting the tension on the rope.
6. Double Figure Eight. This is the knot used for tying into a rope for climbing. The Walker probably won't have to do any climbing, but this is a great knot to know just in case.

So fresh.

So clean.

XI. Hygiene

Hygiene on the road is a challenge. Walkers grow accustomed to being dirty and smelling *awful*. But with just a little determination, a Walker can stay *pretty* clean—at least clean enough to not get nasty infections and die.

There are three areas of the body that a Walker should make every effort to clean *every day*. These are: all the bits between your legs, mouth, and feet. Sadly, not in that order.

I'm not going to tell you *how* to clean yourself. You should know that. But I do have quite a few useful tips.

* * *

As for mouth hygiene, floss every day and try to brush as often as possible.

Cut a toothbrush in half to save weight; carry small tubes of toothpaste to save weight; truly hardcore Walkers should make tooth cleaning powder out of baking soda and salt, which is much lighter than toothpaste and does a pretty good job.

Dental floss is lightweight and doesn't take up much space; in a pinch, you can use it as twine. Walkers should try to floss every day or as often as possible. In general, and specifically due to the high percentage of carbohydrates in a Walker's diet, flossing is probably more important than brushing.

I wish I'd paid more attention to my own advice on this topic when I walked. C'est la vie.

* * *

Best practice is to thoroughly examine the body *every day* for ticks. There will be ticks. If vigilant, Walkers are likely to catch most (if not all) of them before they bite. (Note that Walkers also become hypersensitive to ticklish feelings on the ankles and shins; Walkers catch a lot of these buggers down there.)

Smooth people without much body hair should be able to do this daily tick check pretty easily. Hairy people, on the other hand, have a little more difficulty finding all the ticks. For this reason, I suggest cutting hair short when on a Walk. On my trip, I probably took 50 ticks off of me and about 1000 off of Mabel. However, I was only *actually bitten* by three ticks—one on my stomach, one on my head, and one in my luxurious and powerful beard.

A. The Trucker's Shower

Walkers should learn how to take a trucker's shower. (Some people use another name for this.) This is basically cleaning yourself using only a sink and a washcloth…or paper towels. Or napkins. Or a handkerchief. Or an old t-shirt.

Using water from a sink or from a water bottle and a handkerchief, clean (in this order): the face, the feet, under the arms, between the legs, and the backside. IN THAT ORDER! Don't mess up that order. As sick and disgusting as this sounds, *Walkers usually won't be able to do this everyday.* But every effort should be made to do this every day because a Walk will go much more smoothly and Walkers will smell a great deal better.

B. Foot Hygiene

Foot hygiene is probably the most important bit of hygiene on the trip. (Mouth hygiene is a close second.) Walkers should wash the feet as often as practical. If the weather is cold, feet should be washed only when near a heat source so that the feet don't get cold. If the ambient temperature is anywhere below 60 or 65 degrees, then the feet should be dried immediately after washing.

When you walk 10, 20, 30, or 40 miles in a day, your feet take a great pounding. It can cause microscopic tears in the skin or tiny lacerations. It often causes blisters. It sometimes causes open sores. Toenails might fall off if the Walker wears shoes. *Each of these injuries is an invitation for infections.* This is not to mention that Walkers stuff their feet into dirty socks and dirtier, nastier shoes the next day!

* * *

Walkers should use a gentle soap and water on the feet every day. Water alone will do, in the absence of soap. It doesn't take much water to wash your feet. Earlier I mentioned to budget a pint of water a day to clean your feet. A Walker can probably get by with a little less water than that, but a pint is a good rule of thumb.

B(1) Blisters

Prevention, prevention, prevention. Blisters end hikes more frequently than any other injury, but they can be prevented. Once you've got one, there's no quick and effective treatment, there is only time and rest. So prevention is the key.

Walkers should keep socks clean, make sure shoes or sandals fit properly, and wear silk sock liners if possible. Particularly sensitive areas prone to hot spots or blisters should be protected with bandages or with moleskin.

Those who are not familiar with moleskin will be before finishing a cross-country hike. Moleskin is a heavy pile cotton product with adhesive on the back. It comes in pre-cut shapes and also in rolls. For blister treatment, you cut a hole in the middle of the moleskin so that the blister is surrounded by moleskin, but not covered by it. That way, your sock or shoe won't irritate the blister beneath it.

Blisters should be treated immediately with triple antibiotic ointment. If warm enough, Walkers should consider sleeping without a sock on the afflicted foot, too, as it never hurts to let those suckers breathe a little.

M.W.C. 33.1: TIME LOST TO INJURY PREVENTION IS TIME NOT LOST.

A Walker should stop the second he or she feels a hot spot or thinks he or she might be getting a blister. Treat the afflicted spot immediately and take steps to prevent aggravating the spot.

C. Washing Clothes

Hahahahah! HAHAHAHAHAHA! (Take a breath.) HAHAHAHAHAHA!

Walkers have few clothes that they wear all the time in extreme conditions and they are usually dirty. A Walker's clothes are usually dirtier than any clothes you have ever worn before. They will be covered in dirt and grime and salt. They will smell bad.

For much of my Walk, the weather was very hot and I sweat through my shirts and shorts. Sweat contains salt. The sweat would evaporate, leaving behind the salt. So most of my dark colored hiking shirts and my dark colored shorts developed what looked like white tie-dye patterns in salt stains. That's sexy, I know. But that's just how glamorous it is out there.

There is inconsistent access to laundry facilities on a Walk. Walkers become so accustomed to wearing disgusting clothes that sometimes Walkers will forego doing laundry in order to save time. The only exception to this is with socks—they should be washed at every chance.

* * *

The cheapest, easiest, and fastest way to do laundry on the road is to wash clothes in a sink before bed. This can be done in all motels and in some campgrounds. To do this, draw a few cups of warm or hot water in a sink and add a touch of liquid soap. (Any kind of soap will do.) Plunge the offending garment into the water until it is soaked, and then squeeze out the soap and water. Plunge it in again and, while it is soaked with soap and water, rub the piece of clothing against itself using both hands. Do this liberally and intensely on problem areas. Then squeeze out the water and repeat. Then draw clean water into the sink and rinse the garment.

This process is shocking and disgusting the first time, and it gives a person perspective on life. After several hundred miles on dusty roads, clothes will be noticeably lighter after washed. The washing water will be dark brown to black after the first few rinses.

Keep in mind that people all over the planet do laundry this way every day.

D. Camp Soap, Tooth Paste, Etc.

The Walker should carry soap and tooth paste. This is a highly personal area—everyone has different needs and wants for hygiene products.

First, the lightest weight camp soap comes in little strips that look like paper. You put a piece in your hand, add water, and voila! Those little strips are actually soap! I used this before and after each meal and then sometimes just for good measure. This was my preferred camp soap because it was light, easy to use, and relatively cheap. Some folks prefer to take a bar of soap along with them. The Seyals did:

> "I suggest Dr. Bronner's Bar soap. It is more diverse in use than the liquid, but I did not appreciate this until my tent zippers failed the day I met my first camel spider in Utah. No, we did not have zipper lube handy. Bar soap works great as a makeshift zipper lube and can easily be shaved off and dissolved in water to make the familiar diluted liquid version. A bar is also less likely to open unexpectedly and leak all over your stuff. You can use Dr. Bronner's soap for your laundry,

body, face, hair, dishes, as toothpaste (not recommended), and for any other cleaning needs. The tea-tree soap has disinfectant qualities, but know that tea-tree oil is toxic to dogs and should not be used on them."

--John Seyal

Note how John mentioned using a bar of soap as lubrication for a stuck zipper—that's finding multiple uses for things, and the Walker does it all the time. Note also that he mentioned a *bar* of soap and not liquid soap; this is because liquid soap is much heavier, due to moisture content.

I very rarely used soap to clean my dishes.

* * *

For toothpaste, I started the trip with baking soda and salt that I mixed myself with a little peppermint oil. It is lighter and cheaper than toothpaste, but I couldn't make more while on the trip. So I ended up using travel-sized tubes of toothpaste. You can pick them up for free in some motels!

* * *

M.W.C. 41.2: TRY TO MAKE A GOOD IMPRESSION.

Walkers should carry a travel-sized bottle of mouthwash and a high-powered deodorant just in case he or she has to make a "good impression". A few times on the trip, Walkers may have to meet with people in stores, or maybe media people, or just someone who you would rather meet not smelling like a horse smells. In these instances, it's good to have a little mouthwash and deodorant handy. I actually carried with me a very small can of that awful, horrible, nasty body spray that smells like a junior high boys' locker room. In real life that stuff is nasty, but it will cover up your road stench with a more socially acceptable stench.

E. Asuntos de las Mujeres

Men, feel free to skip this section. This is the women's hygiene section.

Women's hygiene issues? Wait…you're not telling me that *women* can hike across the United States? Shouldn't they be at home, scared, learning to knit? Nonsense! Women are awesome and are better at almost everything than men.

M.W.C. 6: It would be better if women ran the world; everyone would have a lot more fun.

I have no first-person experience with this material, so I asked Kait Seyal to help out. I also asked a doctor I know, who has asked to remain anonymous and whom we will call "The Doctor". The Doctor tells me that I am obligated to say something like this: Women should consult with their gyno and/or primary care physical prior to beginning a cross-country hike in order to discuss options that are available to assist in managing menstrual cycles.

Club 3200 member Kait Whistler Seyal, what say you?

"Ok lady, so you want to walk across America. Yes, women can and do walk across continents. Training, gear, and concerns of your average woman will be the same as your average man. Except that one…little…thing. Yes ladies, we're going to talk about periods. Gentlemen, please feel free to skip ahead.

"We all have our own way, but extreme circumstances sometimes call for extreme measures. As with everything else in my life leading up to the walk, I did a deep examination of my period as a life's practice. In the name of minimalism and hygiene, I had to change my ways. I am a new woman, never to return to the mistakes of my past.

"First, let's rule out some options. Pads and Tampons have a few common problems. They take a significant amount of space to carry. The waste generated is bulky and not biodegradable, so you will have to carry it with you until you can properly dispose of it. Blood, like food waste, can attract animals. In action, pads won't stay put while you are walking all day. Imagine real life diaper rash on your adult nether regions. And lets be honest: The odor can become a problem. Tampons take up less space, but only if you get the kind without an applicator. Tampons can change the PH in your body and as we know, cotton grows bacteria. Lets use some logic. We already know not to buy cotton clothing for this journey. The same logic applies with your female sanitation products. When you already know you will not be clean by any stretch of the imagination, don't provide a place for bacteria to grow. Tampons can also cause TSS – toxic shock syndrome. If you don't know what this is, look it up. It's ugly, potentially fatal, and not something you want to risk on the road. Like I said, I decided I needed to change things up for the walk.

"I needed two special things to manage my periods: flushable baby wipes (with numerous other uses), and a menstrual cup. The baby wipes could go without saying, but when it comes to keeping your lady bits clean, whatever part of your cycle you happen to be on, there is no substitute. Make sure they are flushable to ensure they are easy to dispose of and will break down.

"A menstrual cup is a soft cone-shaped cup that catches, rather than absorbs, menstrual blood. Think "oil pan". They can be disposable or reusable. You only have to carry one of them and there is little to no waste (aside from the baby wipes).

"I used a DivaCup and other women have recommended the Mooncup. Their websites have great information if you have any questions about sanitation, use, and care. Initially, this product will cost you about $30-50, but you won't have to stop by the pharmacy in the next few days to restock. With a single purchase, you are fully equipped for the next 12 months. Soft Cup, a disposable and far less expensive option, is great if you want to try a similar product before investing in a re-usable cup.

"There is a learning curve (remember learning how to use a tampon?) and I suggest using a liner for a little extra insurance while you're getting used to it. I would consider adding, "Get to know my menstrual cup" to your list of things to do before you begin your walk.

"Manage your period the same way you would manage any other private practice. Empty the cup in a cat hole or toilet as is standard with bodily waste, and dispose of your paper waste as usual. Done. No big deal.

"One final note of vital importance: Make sure your hands are clean when handling your lady business. Keep that kitten clean!"

--Kait Seyal

Is there any thing whereof it may be said, See, this is new? It hath been already of old time, which was before us.

XII. Little Things

The real lessons begin once the Walker finally gets out on the road—the Walker learns a million little things. He or she invents new uses for old items. It's quite amazing. The problem is that a lot of this information doesn't fit neatly into any particular category of information. This chapter contains a few of those things.

* * *

Most of the tips in this chapter fall under this heading:

M.W.C. 27: Use what you have.

Club 3200 member Nate Damm is the first person I heard to articulate this philosophy in this way: "Use what you have." I think it is a spot-on explanation of part of the mindset of the cross-country hiker. I'll let Mr. Damm explain:

> "This is a weird motto I came up with on the walk, which is kind of hard to explain: Use what you have. But it makes sense in my weird brain. Anyway, basically, if someone offers you a candy bar, take the damn candy bar. Don't think 'oh, there's a store up ahead, I'll want a candy bar more then and I'm kind of full from breakfast' and then get there and see the store doesn't exist. That sucks.
>
> "Same goes with water. Top your bottles off constantly. Or if you slightly have to take a shit and are at a gas station that has a bathroom, take the shit there. Don't think that you will find a place in the woods later or bask in the glory of a full sized Wal-Mart bathroom later on, only to stumble into a residential area and have to go RIGHT NOW and have to squat under a filthy, very low bridge near a bunch of houses

and hope that nobody sees you. That may or may not have happened to me."

--Nate Damm

A. All the Little Bags

One of your greatest strengths on the road is organization within a pack or cart. The Walker usually wants items organized neatly and with some rational system of order so that the right item can be had quickly with minimal fumbling and searching. The best way to accomplish this is to use a lot of little bags. They call these things "stuff sacks", or "ditty sacks". Call them whatever you want.

Best practice is to organize gear by type, by use, or by the time of day particular equipment is needed, and to store it all accordingly in different colored bags. For example, keep fire lighting tools and tinder in a red bag, signifying that it is the "fire bag". Or water purification equipment can all go into a blue bag. You get the idea. The goal is to be able to identify quickly what you are looking for.

The Walker should keep all go-to equipment handy at all times so that there's always quick and easy access to important items like a flashlight, phone, knife, or whatever it is that a hiker might always need access to.

M.W.C. 46.2: ORGANIZATION MAKES A SLOW JOB FASTER.

Walkers should designate a medium-sized stuff sack as a "tent sack" and fill it with all of the items that are needed in the tent at night. Walkers should learn to recognize this particular sack by look *and* by texture, so that it can be identified by feel inside the pack or cart at night. This will greatly speed up camp set up, especially at night—pitch your tent, toss in the "tent sack", cover equipment, and you're golden. Here is what I kept in my tent sack: flashlight, toilet paper, bear spray, notebook, travel alarm, Kindle, a cheap battery operated lantern. Grab that bag and, Boom! You're in bed.

B. Storage: The Duct Tape Case Study

The more uses an item has, the greater the utility of that single item.

M.W.C. 27.1: Find multiple uses for things.

Many items can be cross-purposed for storage.

Let's consider duct tape, for example: Duct tape comes in handy all of the time. Everyone knows this. In a pinch, you can use duct tape to mend tents, tarps, umbrellas, and even clothing. The trick is how to carry duct tape with you, because you won't need a whole enormous roll of it.

I say: Wrap your water bottle with a couple layers of duct tap; it will insulate the water bottle a little bit and is a space efficient way to carry it.

And well, well, well, looky here: Young John Seyal thinks he knows better than I do how to carry duct tape. He says:

> "Wrap it longways around an old credit card and toss it in your pack. You can carry quite a bit of duct tape in an area the size of a deck of cards this way."
> --John Seyal

Well. Yeah. Well. Ok...yeah, that's a pretty good idea. Seyal wins this round.

C. The Power of the Handkerchief

Handkerchiefs are amazing. Some people call them bandanas. I'll allow that. These little squares of fabric have many uses.

* * *

One of the best ways to cool down in the hot, hot Sun is to wear a wet handkerchief on the head. The water in the handkerchief evaporates and draws heat away from the body, the same way that sweat does, but on a larger scale. There are any number of ways to do this, but I favor the Modified Kerchief Bandana Method, or the "MKBM". It goes like this:

Prepare two adjoining corners of a handkerchief by twisting the corners and putting a simple overhand knot in each corner, leaving little tails of an inch or so; place the knotted corners on the backside of your head, one knot on each side of your head. Pull the handkerchief over your head to the front, and then twist the front corners of the handkerchief as you did with the other corners. Instead of tying off the front corners, tie the twisted ends together on the front of your head, again with a simple overhand knot. Soak the handkerchief with water then put on your wide-brimmed hat. BOOM! That's basically a head-fitted air conditioner.

* * *

Using the same science as employed in the MKBM, the Walker can keep a water bottle cool for drinking using a kerchief and extra water. Soak a t-shirt or handkerchief in water and wrap that around a water bottle; the evaporation of the water from the kerchief will cool the water in the water bottle—a little.

* * *

Bandanas make great hobo socks. Hobo socks are especially useful and amazing if the Walker has adopted the sandal-lifestyle, as I've advocated. Here's how to make a simple, long wearing sock that protects the important bits while remaining lightweight and cool:

Fold a bandana into a triangle. Place it on the ground with the fold toward you and the opposite point of the folded triangle pointed away from your body. Place your right foot on the triangle, with the point of the triangle near the ball of the foot. Wrap the folded side of the triangle around the *back* of your heel, just above where the Achilles tendon meets the heel. Tie the two loose ends of the triangle together on the front of the foot, on top of the instep. Don't tie it too tightly. Now slip that little foot into a sandal.

If you've done it right, the bandana should protect the heel (which often needs protection from blisters), as well as the moving, articulated parts of the side of the ankle. Adjust the bandana on the instep of the foot so that it protects the foot from 1) the strap of the sandal, and 2) the Sun.

This will help prevent the sandal strap cutting into the foot and will greatly reduce sunburn on the top of the foot. At the same time, it allows a great deal of heat to escape from the foot.

(Of all the things I "invented" when I walked across America, this hobo sock method was probably the most popular among other hikers. I've heard rave reviews on this. John Seyal and Nate Damm have both endorsed this method. Rave reviews, I tell you!)

D. The PCT Bear Bag Trick

The most versatile way of hanging a bear bag is the PCT bear bag trick. It requires: a bear bag, nylon para cord, a cheap carabiner, and a stick that you pick up off the ground.

Put all your food in the bear bag and close the bag. Clasp the handles of the bear bag together with a carabiner. Tie one end of the para cord around the handles of the bear bag. Toss the other end of the para cord over a tree branch using a rock to weight that end. Thread that end of the para cord through the carabiner, and then pull the bear bag *all the way up to the tree branch*, as high as you can.

Then form a slip hitch knot as high as you can on the para cord and fasten a stick in the hitch. (The stick will have to be thick enough to support the weight of the bear bag.) Finally, lower the bag back toward the ground until the stick reaches and locks on the carabiner. The bag is now securely hung.

This is the best way to hang a bear bag.

You Will Never Walk Alone

XIII. Companions

Is a cross-country hike better solo or with a companion or two? Tough call. Or it would be a tough call, if you had any friends crazy enough to join on a trip like this. This question is usually moot because it's difficult to find more than one person with both the inclination and the time to walk across a continent.

That said, hardly anyone does an entire cross-country walk entirely alone. Almost everyone has a hiking partner for at least part of the trip. I had Mabel with me the whole time! I also had a friend join me across Indiana and later I sort of teamed up with another cross-country hiker.

So the Walker might from time to time have a trail friend out there. Hiking companions can be a blessing or something less than a blessing.

* * *

A cross-country hike puts a great deal of strain on any friendship, intimate relationship, or working relationship. This is because cross-country hiking is a hybrid between a lifestyle and a job, so hiking partners on a cross-country hike sometimes must interact like friends and sometimes like colleagues, work buddies, business partners. The Walk is, at its core, a *solo* practice, so teamwork is not usually supremely important, but *communication* is vitally important.

This is a long way of saying that hiking with a partner requires effort to maintain a working relationship. People hike at different speeds, break naturally at different intervals, and have different natural sleeping patterns. One person may want to hit the road before sunrise every morning and pitch camp by 4; one person may want to sleep until 7 and hike until 8. Any difference in hiking style, no matter how small, will potentially put strain on the relationship and will require one or both of the partners to give a little.

Best practice in avoiding potential problems is through communication and expectation management. Be courteous, but be clear about what you expect from any potential hiking partners. Just as importantly, be clear *and honest* when a potential hiker expresses expectations to you.

A. Car Support

Car support is great. It makes the trip a lot more enjoyable in a lot of ways because it minimizes many of the dangers inherent in the trip. On the other hand, it also puts a lot more responsibility on whoever is primarily responsible for planning the trip. I had Mabel with me, so I knew that I would have to have car support in the deserts of the Southwest. But a solo hike, or a hike with just one or two human people, probably doesn't *require* car support.

At any rate, car support is *not* necessary at least until the western slope of the Rocky Mountains. The hiking is difficult in western Nebraska/Kansas where Walkers hit the first long stretches without water, but nothing that can't be handled with a cart and good planning. But lack of water in Western Colorado and Utah presents serious danger. And Nevada? Nevada is three times the size of Canada and there is no running water in the entire state. There are only three wells, and two of those wells are controlled by Bedouin tribes that don't allow outsiders to drink.

A(1) Car Support Concerns

Car support is *expensive*. The car adds the substantial additional cost of gasoline as well as living expenses for the driver. So car support can really cramp a budget.

* * *

The first job of the support car is to carry extra equipment and to hang around in the vicinity of a Walker in case of bear attack or snakebite. It is also available for high-adventure rescue missions when the Walker is abducted and held for ransom by proto-fascist separatist political parties. Obviously, these things very rarely happen.

So the support car tends to function as a repository of extra equipment, a scout, a resupply agent, and an occasional lift off trail to a motel when camping can't be secured. The added sense of security is great, but in absence of any actual emergency, the most visible benefits of car support are: 1) greatly increased hiking speed due to smaller hiking loads and faster resupply, and 2) another person or two to hang around with at night around a fire.

* * *

A 4 x 4 isn't necessary, but the right kind of car is. Depending on the number of hikers, the number of support folks, and the amount of equipment, a compact car might not do the trick. Most people I know who have used car support have used some sort of small SUV or station wagon. The Subaru Outback seems to be the most popular (naturally). But I was on a budget, so I couldn't buy a car. I borrowed a car from a friend—a Toyota Corolla. It did the trick, but it was a little bit cramped for our party.

The car should in all cases be a four-door model and should, to the extent possible, get decent gas mileage. As mentioned, the car support tends to function primarily as a scout and resupply car, so the mileage can add up.

The car doesn't need to be an F-250 with a 12-inch lift kit and 36-inch Super Swamper tires, but the higher the clearance, the better. Once west of the Mississippi, if not before, Walkers often use back roads, gravel roads, dirt roads, and the like. Additionally, campsites are sometimes *less than paved*. For these reasons, it's best to have a little bit of clearance and for the driver to have a little bit of experience driving in unpaved conditions.

Note that there are roads in the Southwest that aren't passable even by 4 x 4 vehicle. There are paved roads around these problem areas, but it's something to be aware of.

* * *

The support car must *always* have a spare tire that has air in it.

All other standard practices are encouraged, of course—fluids should be checked each time it's gassed up, lights and turn signals tested, etc. But Walkers should not forget the spare tire because there will be flat tires.

Sounds like common sense, I know. But you'd be surprised how scarce a commodity common sense is in this day and age.

* * *

Car support requires communication abilities. This is generally not a problem because everyone has cell phones these days. But car and Walker must be able to get into contact at any given moment. There are high-powered hand-held radios that will work for this, too, but they are not worth the expense or the weight if everyone has a cell phone, anyway.

Communication is required for two reasons: 1) obviously, if a Walker needs some assistance, he or she has to be able to call the car, and 2) there are places (usually in the Southwest), where impassable roads will require a Walker and the car to separate along different roads. In the latter case, it's vitally important to have communication capabilities in order to reconvene at a later point.

* * *

The last concern worth mentioning is sheer boredom. It's not easy to find a driver who can handle the boredom of doing nothing all day long except driving five or ten miles, waiting, then driving five or ten more miles...and then waiting again. Then driving five or ten miles and...you get the idea. A support car driver must be a very laid-back and self-sufficient type.

Kait Seyal agrees. She says: "Someone working on their novel or a musician working on their album (like our amazing one-man support team, Jon) are ideal. When a driver gets bored, they might want to start solving "problems." But after only a few weeks on the road, a successful cross-country hiker learns that there are very few true problems in life. The rest of the "problems" are just drama that people invent (often subconsciously) to entertain themselves. You do not need one of these "problem solvers" driving your support car."

A(2) Car Support Concerns

Car support is *expensive*—and I'm not sure about it. If I had to do the Walk again but in a short period of time, I'd want car support. The camaraderie is nice and it can potentially speed things up. But it is *expensive*, and it's not necessary for a seasoned hiker with a cart. So I'm not sure where I come down on car support. Here's John Seyal's take:

"Having a sag wagon is expensive, but it's a game changer. Most transcontinental road walkers I know used a sag wagon for at least a portion of their trek. I think of our walk in terms of "pre-car" and "post-car"—that's how big a difference it made. With a chase car comes safety, security, mobility, and a lot of (relative) comfort. However, a support vehicle also brings with it additional responsibilities and, most importantly, *options*.

Kait and I walked 1100 miles without a sag wagon. Once the summer heat ramped up, we called our good friend who had offered to drive for us. He joined us with a car at the Mississippi River and he drove our sag wagon 2000 miles, all the way to the Pacific. (Thanks, Jon. You are an amazing friend.)

Kait and I had considered a support vehicle before our walk. Our project was focused around our dogs and their volunteer work, so we had to ensure their safety and comfort; we talked and thought with deeply furrowed brows about having a car to carry the dogs through the Midwest heat. Eventually, we decided that we could start without a support car and we would re-approach the idea if we ran into trouble. As soon as we started to plan, we lost all interest in having a car. I took great pride in the idea of being out there all alone—*Roughing it*! I started thinking of the chase car as a big gas-guzzling ball and chain.

A sag wagon is great, but it costs two of the most transformative elements of this kind of pilgrimage: Uncertainty and Simplicity.

Imagine the following completely realistic road scenario: You have been walking all day. Your feet are shredded and blistered beyond recognition. You are almost out of water and food. The Sun is going down and you are still five miles from the next town and it is starting to rain, and you don't know where you can sleep safely and your backpack is really damn heavy. What do you do?

If you are on foot without support, you are stranded—in the best way possible. Awareness of how exposed you are informs every decision. Without support, dangers are more real and options are limited, and that makes decision-making a surprisingly simple process. You either commit to walking through rain and dark and hope you can find shelter in town; or, you suck it up, pitch a tent in the next best spot to get out of the rain, sleep hungry, and crush the last five miles in the morning. Pretty simple, right?

Now imagine that same scenario, but this time you have a friend in a support car waiting for you in the town ahead. Now, you could tough it out and camp in the rain, or slog five miles in cold and dark. Or, your car could pick you up and take you ahead or back to anywhere: A city park, a friendly yard, a motel with beds and showers, home; the options are endless and inviting. Guaranteed, you will take the first chance you have to get driven two miles out of your way for a hot meal; but deciding to walk two miles off-trail—and then two more miles back—for that same meal is an entirely different kind of decision.

This is the most critical trade-off with a support car: It gives you more options and overcomplicates the simple challenges of a nomadic lifestyle. No matter what you gain by having a car, you will lose the unique sense of isolation and *Freedom!* that comes with living out of a backpack. It's really not much different than a road-trip in everyday life before the walk, except that you move much slower and work a lot harder.

I wouldn't encourage or discourage anyone from choosing to walk with support. It was right for our project, but if I could do it again I would make every effort to not need a sag wagon at all. If we had not been walking with our dogs, we would have never had a car. I would never trade those first 1100 car-less miles; but in the end, our decision was the right one for our project. Without our sag wagon, we would not have been able to continue volunteering with our dogs and our cause would have been dead in the water. Without a sag wagon we would not have been able to adopt a wonderful homeless dog in the farmlands of Iowa. And without a sag wagon, we would not have been able to give a fellow traveler a ride that turned into a five-week odyssey of self-discovery and cultural exchange. He's a lifelong friend now, all because we had a sag wagon. True story."

B. Couples

Quite a few people are tempted to become Couple Walkers. I walked solo (and my Walk was partially responsible for ending a relationship I was in at the time), so I'm not the best to talk on this subject. Old Nate Damm walked solo, too. Still, when I finished my

Walk and had the benefit of some experience, I called up John and Kait Seyal, who were just about to begin their Walk. I said, "You know, this could destroy your marriage...or it could make your marriage stronger, I guess?" I just wanted them to understand that there would be a lot of stress on their relationship. Every potential Walker should know that.

Hey, Kait Seyal...tell me some stuff:

"On a brief visit home during our walk for my grandmother's funeral, I told my father that even if he didn't fully understand the walk, that I hoped he could see at least some value in what we were doing. He didn't comment, as I expected him to, on the value of our volunteer work or our renewed sense of faith in our country and its people. He told me that John and I were making an invaluable investment in our marriage that would serve us well for the rest of our lives. My dad is a smart man.

"It doesn't matter how long you've known your partner or how well you think you know each other. You will learn more about your SO than you ever wanted to know, hand in hand with the things you are learning about yourselves. Make no mistake, this will make or break your relationship. Be ready for it. If you aren't ready or willing to face the deepest, darkest corners of every aspect of your relationship, then this is not something you two need to do together.

"You will learn absolute truth and then have to decide what to do with it. On the bright side, you'll have lots of time to talk and work though things as they come up. And they will.

"John and I benefited deeply from taking this journey together. We had our bumps (by bumps, I mean arguments and screaming matches in the middle of an empty desert) but we used them as opportunities to rebuild and grow stronger from them. Our marriage and friendship has never been stronger."

C. Don't Take a Dog, Unless You Absolutely Have To

Walkers are encouraged *not* to take a pet along on a Walk. I took Mabel and she loved it. But a pet is a *huge* responsibility. With a dog, hiking days are lost to cold and to hot weather that would not stop a human hiker. A dog adds a lot of extra weight in dog food and supplies. A dog requires a lot of grooming and trips to the vet. It's a *huge* responsibility.

It's just...it's a lot of responsibility, and I worry about dogs. Don't get me wrong, Mabel and I had a great time together and she's sitting at my feet right now as I type this. But I made thousands of concessions for her safety. And I was able to arrange car support in the Southwest where it would not be safe for a dog to walk a thousand miles due to heat and salt on their little puppy paws.

Most pet owners—even *great* pet owners—probably don't have what it takes to handle a cross-country hike with a dog. In the end, it's a personal decision, but it's not one to be taken lightly.

* * *

Plus, the Walker who takes a dog should be prepared to get hate mail about how he or she is "abusing" the dog. I advise against taking a dog for practical reasons, but not because I assume a cross-country hike to be "abusive". Quite the contrary. John and Kait Seyal received emails like this when they walked across with their therapy dogs, too. I imagine it was infuriating to them, too.

The dog's safety has to be a priority. When you spend every hour of every day, day in and day out, worrying about the safety of your best friend, it's *infuriating* when some desk-bound bloviating flat head accuses you of abusing your best friend. It causes one to anger.

Let me make this absolutely clear: Even though I suggest not taking a dog, for convenience and practical reasons, it is just about the happiest existence possible for a dog. The closest thing to "abuse" about it is that I brought Mabel back to a regular housedog lifestyle after the Walk ended—a lifestyle probably not unlike that of most of the schmucks who think that a dog hiking across America is abuse.

* * *

John and Kait Seyal started their Walk with two dogs, added a third along with their support car driver, and picked up a fourth off the highway in Iowa. Therapy dogs were the core of their project, so they have a great deal to say about the subject.

[*Editor's Note*: John and Kait Seyal contributed most of the material in the remainder of this section. I edited this for them, and where I have additions, I will mark them off with brackets. Otherwise, take it away, Seyals....]

C(1) The Pros of Taking a Pup

There are a number of pros associated with taking a dog on a Walk:

- Love and comfort; they will make you smile.
- They help you stay warm on cold nights.
- They are a strong deterrent to anyone who might consider messing with you and are a good alarm system should any creature walk into your camp at night.
- They will help you meet people and will tell you how they feel about people.
- Keeping them safe will often help keep you safe as well. For example, "No, your dog can't walk across that railroad bridge. Well, I guess you can't either."

C(1)(a) The Cons of Taking a Pup

Yeah...but there are also a number of really important cons. Let's be realistic: Bringing a dog is a huge responsibility and commitment. Kait says: "Tyler told us that 'they will slow you down.

A lot.' And we believed him, but we had no idea how right he really was."

Humans are tougher than dogs on any long distance hike: faster, stronger, more endurance, less affected by heat, rain, or cold, and able to carry more weight. You say, "You've never met my hyper-as-all-get-out dog." I promise you, it doesn't matter. Even *your* dog will eventually run out of gas. You will be carrying food and extra water for them as well, so consider the added weight you are taking on.

They will not be able to carry all of their own stuff and keep up with you. Period. They will not be allowed in certain areas you need to go. If you go into a grocery store, what will you do with your dog? Can they be left unattended? There is also the liability to consider as well, but more on that later.

If a Walker chooses to take a dog, the Walker takes on full responsibility for the overall health, safety, and general quality of life for that pup. Do not take this lightly.

C(2)(a) Training

The behavior of a Walker's dog reflects on the Walker. And Walkers with dogs are potentially personally liable for anything or anyone the dog damages. If your dog bites someone, regardless of who is at fault, the person can likely sue you, and that will be expensive. It's a legal and ethical issue. And the law is never in favor of the dog owner—so don't take a dangerous dog, and manage the dog you take.

The best preparation you can give your dog is to take them anywhere you can. Find a dog-friendly patio where you can go for a coffee or lunch. How romantically French, oui? Take them for a car ride when you run errands. We take the dogs to the bank (believe it or not, most of them are accepting of well-mannered dogs), the hardware store, the bookstore, the farmer's market, etc. Of course, always ask before you bring a dog into any store. You might be surprised by how many say yes. Just make sure they're ready to handle the outing. Start with something easy like a pet supply store.

* * *

A cross-country dog needs to have some basic things down before a journey like this. They need to walk politely on a leash at the heel. They should also know they basic sit, stay (when tied to the cart, pack, etc.), and the ever-important recall. If your dog does nothing else, make sure they come when called. A dog's basic obedience is invaluable.

They need to be comfortable with other dogs because people with dogs will likely host Walkers. So the Walker should not have a dog-aggressive dog. Again, a Walker will likely be personally liable for any damage caused by his or her dog.

A cross-country dog must be house trained, and even house-trained dogs must be watched very closely in any new environment. Don't let them pee on anyone's couch.

C(3)(a)(i) Physical

A dog on a cross-country hike must be fit and their feet need to be tough. A Walk is mostly on roads, so dogs must be trained on roads and sidewalks. Best practice is to start small and slowly increase miles, watching carefully for signs of wear, soreness and fatigue. A Walker should *not* depend on boots to protect their dog's feet. Dog booties cannot always be used due to heat and other factors.

C(3)(b) Medical

No one should take a dog on a cross-country hike without first taking the dog to the veterinarian. It is best (and required) practice to see the vet, tell them the plan, and ask their opinion. The Walker must listen very carefully to the vet's opinion and should follow their vet's advice.

C(3)(b)(i) Vaccines, Maintenance Medication

A cross-country dog must be up-to-date on all vaccines and wellness exams and must have a clean bill of health.

The vaccination against leptospirosis is optional for most dogs; it's best practice, and potentially required, for a cross-country dog. You and your dog will be sharing the great outdoors with wild animals. It's worth it.

* * *

Cross-country dogs must be on flea, tick, heartworm, and intestinal parasite preventative. This may be topical parasite control, like Frontline, and separate intestinal and heartworm meds, or an all-encompassing product like trifexis. But dogs *must* be protected against parasites. It is the dog owner's responsibility to keep the dog healthy and safe. And, on a Walk, if the dog has bugs…you have bugs. Yes, it costs money. If you can't afford it, don't take your dog.

Repeat: **If you cannot afford it, don't take a dog.**

C(3)(b)(ii) Vet Visits

We took our dogs to the vet before their Walk, during their Walk, and after they finished their Walk. We took them in for an appointment about every 1,000 miles just to make sure everyone was doing well. Even if all you get is a pat on the back and the assurance that you are doing a good job, the peace of mind is worth the $40 vet visit.

C(3)(b)(iii) Dog First Aid

The American Red Cross offers a First Aid for Pets class that focuses on emergency first aid for dogs and cats. Best practice for a Walker with a pet is to take this course.

C(4) Special Equipment

Walkers with dogs need a secondary list of necessary equipment. Dogs can carry some things some of the time. But the decision to bring a dog adds weight to the Walker's pack as well.

C(4)(a) Dog Packs

Dog packs are not appropriate for all dogs, but are helpful if the dog is amenable to it. There are a number of affordable, quality dog packs available. It is crucial that any equipment they wear fits properly.

The heavier the dog pack, the fewer miles the dog can cover. Dogs are inefficient pack animals and carrying a pack raises the dog's temperature. Dogs wearing packs must be monitored accordingly. As a decent rule of thumb, never put more than 1/10 a dog's weight in a dog pack.

C(4)(b) Puppy Paws

Cross-country dogs should be trained on pavement to help toughen up their feet for the road. Watch for unevenness in their gait and check your pal's feet every time you take a break. Dogs have a much more intimate relationship with the ground than shod humans and different surfaces affect their feet in different ways, so the Walker should be vigilant in examining paws.

C(4)(b)(i) Dog Boots

[*Author's Note:* I just wanted to say that I don't believe in dog boots. I think they are bad, except in the limited case of taking a dog for a walk in the winter on salted sidewalks. If pavement or rock is too hot for a dog's paws, then it's too hot for a dog's paws and the dog shouldn't be on the pavement—boots are awful in those circumstances. Ok! Back to the Seyals.]

A dog loses heat from its body two ways: by panting and by sweating through the pads of their feet. Boots can be great in the snow or in cool weather, but forget it in the heat. Boots will cause a dog's feet to sweat and cause chafing. A dog could overheat very easily because the boots don't breathe.

Instead, baby socks can provide a barrier against hot pavement while still allowing pads to sweat, breathe, and dissipate heat. They are a nice alternative to boots in warm weather. It's possible to affix baby socks to a dog's paws using flexible tape, vet wrap, or sports tape just below the knee. Tape should not be wrapped too tightly, or else it might restrict circulation.

It's even more important to check the dog's feet often if the pup is wearing baby socks. If it's too hot to walk without socks, they probably shouldn't be walking. If the dog is more comfortable with baby socks on, it's worth a shot, but you need to keep an eye out for overheating.

C(4)(b)(ii) Bag Balm

Bag balm is great for massaging into sore, cracked pads. Bag balm (sometimes called udder balm) is non-toxic, old-tymey, and can be found anywhere. It ain't bad on human hands and feet either.

C(4)(b)(iii) Dog Dishes

A cross-country dog needs his or her own food dish. There are fancy collapsible models, but any lightweight dish will do. [*Author's Note*: Seriously, *any* lightweight dish will do. I bought a collapsible bowl for the trip and, when I lost it, I replaced it with a microwave soup dish. It worked exactly as well.]

C(4)(c) Dog Meds

The Walker should pack the dog's monthly prescription meds, as discussed above. The Walker should carry several months' worth because prescription meds can only be obtained from a vet that has seen the dog. Walkers with dogs should plan on a single mid-trip refill, or have friends mail meds to them on the road.

C(4)(d) Tags

A Walker's dog should wear two tags: 1) a rabies vaccine tag, and 2) a nametag with the owner's contact information and contact information for another trusted friend/relative in case the Walker cannot be reached. Best practice is also to have a cross-country dog micro-chipped so that they can be identified and returned even if they lose their collar.

C(5) Diet

A Walker should talk to his or her vet and research diet options. Walkers cannot always count on having access to the same type/brand of dog food, so some Walkers may have to plan ahead if they have dogs with sensitive stomachs. Mixing old and new food together helps ease the transition from one type of food to another. Take diet seriously and watch for signs of malnutrition.

C(6) Know Your Dog

Every dog is different and what is normal for one dog could be an early sign of a problem for others.

The Walker must know when to rest. A dog will get tired and hot before a human. A Walker with a dog is choosing to let the dog's limits set the pace. Dogs are loyal and they love you more than anything. They will follow you anywhere; so don't expect them to tell you when they need to stop. It is *the Walker's responsibility* to know when their dog must rest. Know the signs of canine heat exhaustion. Know how to cool them down fast. You should never let your dog get to this point.

[*Author's Note*: Tyler again. Quick note on a tip from the road: If a dog gets overheated, or appears to be close to overheating and is having difficulty cooling down, a really quick way to help them out is to soak a cloth with alcohol and dab it on their paws and ears. Alcohol evaporates much faster than water—that's why it feels cool when you put alcohol on your skin. The rapid evaporation will help the pup to dissipate heat and to cool its blood.]

C(6)(b) Lighten Their Load

The lighter your dog's load, the more miles they will be able to cover. A walker might absorb the dog's pack into his or her own and take on the weight themselves, as Tyler Coulson did for the first half of his hike with Mabel. But an even better plan is to get a cart.

Walkers with dogs who can afford car support should get car support. If a dog cannot walk the miles you want to cover, you can call in a support car so that they can safely remain on the road with you. Due to the additional expense, this may not be an option.

We got the cart and then support car specifically for the dogs. Without the dogs, we would not have needed the support car. The dogs were so important to our trip that we decided we would do what was necessary for them to stay safe and happy with us—Coulson did that, as well. It meant providing a car and nanny for the dogs. They walked when it was safe and rode when it wasn't. All four of our dogs had a wonderful trip and loved every moment of it.

* * *

Walkers with dogs will often have to *walk less*, or limit their hiking to the cooler hours in the morning and evening. Early morning hiking avoids all the heat radiating off pavement, which is brutal for a dog. Walking at night achieves the same thing, though not as safely due to visibility concerns. Note that walking at night is dangerous—many animals are more active at night, snakes often lay in the road after dark because it is still warm from cooking in the sun all day, and drivers can't see as well. So it ain't exactly safe to walk at night.

Given all these limitations and difficulties, it's important to….

C(6)(c) Know When To Send Your Pup Home

The Walker with a dog must repeat this mantra: "I know and accept that, by bringing my dog on a walk across America, I am agreeing to let the dog set the pace." Most Walkers with dogs will reach a point when it is necessary to make a critical decision, probably due to the heat: Walkers might well decide that everyone is better off continuing without their faithful canine companion, however painful it may be to send them home. Before beginning a Walk, each Walker should make sure to have a friend or family member that is willing to look after the dog for the remainder of your hike should the occasion arise.

D. Hiking Partners?

Hiking with a buddy—*i.e.* neither a romantic partner nor a pet—can be a great life experience. But it can easily go the other way, too. There is tremendous pressure to maintain a hiking partnership once one starts, even if it's a bad partnership, so potential Walkers should be wary about entering any agreements. Hiking partners on a cross-country hike should make damn sure ahead of time that they can get along under stressful conditions, because conditions can (and likely will) be stressful. Unfortunately, it's not really possible to simulate the stresses of a cross-country hike ahead of time.

Out there, hikers see the absolute worst in people. No matter if the partners are married, or a son and child, brothers or sisters, or the oldest of friends—the *other* person will make a million mind bogglingly stupid mistakes. Some of the mistakes will be so mind-bogglingly stupid that you will wonder how the person managed not to kill himself as a child.

The kicker there is that you are the *other* person sometimes. Everyone makes stupid mistakes. Remember that.

* * *

But hiking partners also see the very best the other has to offer. This is just the nature of stressful conditions—you begin to see the best and the worst and just accept the bits in the middle.

I'd say that the added safety and companionship of hiking partners probably outweighs the potential for negatives. But it's best to apply the roommate rule: Hiking partners on a cross-country hike should be the oldest of friends or the newest of strangers; they should be OK with the idea of not being friends at all after the trip, because that might happen. And each and every hiking partner needs to be equal in terms of budgetary expectations and physical expectations.

Llorando

XIV. Brain Matters

If you've made it this far into this book, then you're likely serious about walking across a continent. I haven't convinced you to stay home or to pick an easier hike. You're going to try this thing. I hear you. I get it.

Let's get serious, then.

The stuff that goes on in the mind of the Walker before, during, and after a transcontinental walk is probably the most important aspect of the adventure. It's also the least talked about, the least written about. It's embarrassing stuff because some people think it shows weakness or something. It doesn't.

A. Loneliness and Aloneness

Walkers should prepare for a great deal of loneliness on a cross-country hike. After weeks and weeks on the road, there is a real difference between *aloneness* and *loneliness*—aloneness is just being alone, but loneliness is the longing to be with other people. It's very difficult to prepare or to train for this type of loneliness.

I twice went three days without *seeing* another person, let alone talking with anyone. There were whole weeks in which I didn't have a meaningful conversation with anyone. In these times, I would often stop at every gas station I saw and buy some little thing, like a pack of gum, just to have a conversation with the person behind the counter.

Loneliness will drive you mad unless you give it a hug. The Walker should remember that loneliness is passing and that it is an incredible opportunity to learn, to read, to see things. It's best not to dwell on loneliness when on a Walk.

* * *

Here's what Nate Damm has to say about loneliness:

"When you are walking across America, especially if you are traveling alone, you are going to feel lonely. And I don't mean 'I can't believe nobody showed up to my party' lonely. I mean 'collapsing in a heap of tears on the side of the road or walking an extra 10 miles for the day just so you can get to a gas station in the hopes of finding *anyone* to talk to' lonely. There will be days when you do not interact with a single human. Sometimes this will happen multiple days in a row.

"When I was walking, I found that dealing with loneliness was the toughest part of the walk. When it really comes down to it, anyone can walk 20 miles a day. That's the easy part. It's dealing with being alone so much, among other things, that keeps most people from ever doing such a thing.

"The only solution I found for this was to become my own best friend. This sounds like something a person with no friends would say to make themselves feel better, because it *is* something a person with no friends would say to make themselves feel better. When you are on the road, there are extended periods of time when you do not have friends. There will be nobody there for you, and you have the cold, harsh reality that you are alone staring you in the face. Your survival depends on you. You could have all the friends in the world back home, and they could be as supportive as humanly possible, but you still will be, and feel, alone.

"If you hate yourself, then this can clearly create a pretty bad time. I won't go into the various circumstances that led into my walk, but it's safe to say that I didn't like myself much at the time. I thought that I was sort of a dick. So, if you don't like yourself, but are stuck alone with your thoughts for more time than you can even begin to comprehend right now, you need to find a solution. This is why your mindset has to change. It doesn't necessarily have to change before you leave for your walk, but you need to be consciously working on changing the way you view yourself as you do. And in my opinion, most of this change needs to result in a higher level of personal pride.

"Even if you're a jerk and have nothing to speak of in terms of talents, you will need to find a way to take pride in yourself. If you're not proud of what you're doing, you won't be able to do it successfully.

"Every day that you don't quit and go home is yet another reason to keep going. I'm sure there are people who will tell you that your walk is a bad idea or that they don't think you can do it. Keep these naysayers in mind whenever you feel lonely and depressed. Think about the progress you've made, no matter how small it may be, and be proud of the fact that you aren't back in your old life and doing nothing like you were before. You're doing something amazing, even if you don't realize it at the time. Get in the practice of reminding yourself that you are a badass adventurer and that you are living the hell of out of life, which pretty much makes you better than everyone else by default. Most people waste their lives, you are doing something that puts every last ounce of it to use. Everyone admires adventurers, and you should admire yourself *because you are an adventurer*. You're the person that most people want to be deep down, but they don't have the balls to go for it.

"When you start taking pride in what you're doing, you'll probably start feeling pretty cool all of a sudden. You'll start catching a glimpse of your sexy hobo self in a shop window as you walk by, notice your rugged adventurer good looks and stop for a few seconds just to take in the masterpiece that is you. You'll be more confident, which will lead to more interaction with people, which will then lead to newspaper and TV appearances. People will recognize you on the street and ask to take pictures with you. Especially in small town America, you will essentially be the most interesting person in town in each place you walk through.

"After a while, you'll find that you are not lonely anymore, even in scenarios that normally would have made you uncontrollably homesick. You won't brood over your personal problems all day and be miserable like you were at the beginning of your walk. You'll be very laid back, and dare I say, happy. And all of this awesomeness finds its roots in the simple ability to be proud of what you're doing.

"Every walker would probably have different advice about how to deal with the mental struggle that such a trip brings, but these are my thoughts, and what got me through what was the toughest thing I'd done at the time. Loneliness ripped me apart from inside out for the first couple months of my walk, but what I just shared with you is what allowed me to reach the light at the end of the tunnel and emerge into a trip that was enjoyable to the point that each day felt like the best day of my life."

B. Road Madness

Walkers sometimes go a little mad around the Kansas/Nebraska corridor. The Walker has adopted behaviors that would have scared the "old him", the old him who hadn't walked across half a continent. Clothes are dirty and stink; laundry is done in motel sinks. Drivers stare and meet the Walker's mercenary glare. The Walker has patience *and* a short temper, and that is a rare and sometimes unsafe combination. The conditions and the time alone can potentially drive a person to a kind of road madness.

There's no guarantee that this will happen, but there is always a chance. There is no guaranteed way to avoid it, but there are some steps that can make it easier to deal with. Here are some things that I recommend:

1. **Reading**. Down time spent doing nothing or sulking or stewing about matters beyond control is wasted and it just provides time for people to drive themselves crazy. Reading is a way to stay connected with people.
2. **Talking with strangers**. Any friendly stranger is worth talking to for a bit. It's better to talk with a few friendly folks and to not sweat about losing a half an hour or so from the day's hike. Interacting with people reminds us that we're human.
3. **Calling home a lot**. Talking on the phone isn't as good as talking in real life, but it's better than nothing.

After several months on the road the Walker should try to avoid confrontation if at all possible. This is because the Walker has potentially forgotten or dulled the internalized reality that we all live in a modern, civilized world. Out there, people nearly killed me with their cars, they allowed dogs to attack Mabel and me, and they hit me with trash that they tossed from their cars on the highway. They shouted very bad things at me from time to time, many of which were not true but were designed to provoke.

I was able (in most cases) to maintain composure—but it was a struggle.

M.W.C. 2.1: Don't hit anyone with a stout hiking stick unless they swing first.

C. Failure and Quitting

Failure and quitting are *always* options. That's not a very romantic notion, but it's the truth. A lot of cross-country hikers tell themselves that they "never once doubted that they would make it; it just wasn't a question". I've heard quite a few people say that about quite a few things. For some reason, it's not popular to admit that you have doubts about anything. That's a ridiculous cultural trait that we have here in the U.S.

And it doesn't work very well for me. I get by a lot better when I acknowledge my doubts, and certainly when those around me acknowledge their doubts.

Beginning rather early in my hike (right after a disastrous string of failures), I started a routine of asking myself first thing every morning, "Do I quit or do I go on?" This way, each day was mine; I owned each day because each day I'd chosen to stay on the road. It helped me to live in the moment and to experience the hike as a real, immediate thing. I did not think in terms of stories or memories or books or blogs. I thought about today.

E. All the Crying

Again, everyone reacts differently. But one thing that Walkers tend to have in common is all the crying that happens near the end of the trip. I've heard other Walkers tell me that their crying started a week or two before they finished. Some don't cry at all. Most do.

Mine started the day before I finished. I cried a pretty great deal on the day before I finished and pretty much couldn't control it. The crying went on for weeks after that. It was sort of like sneezing—you know how sometimes a sneeze sneaks up on you, and you don't know it's going to happen until right before it does, and as soon as you feel it starting to happen the only thing you can do is run away from people so as not to sneeze on them? It was like that.

Others who I've talked with have had similar experiences. One person I talked with *didn't* have that experience until several weeks after finishing. Then it started.

I never figured out what triggered crying for me. Maybe there were no triggers? At any rate, crying is usually a component of the post-Walk depression; it's nothing to be embarrassed or afraid of, but it's another thing to be aware of.

194

F. Post-Walk Depression

One thing that seems to unite all Walkers is the experience of post-Walk depression. No matter if the individual quits in Ohio or makes it all the way to the sea, whether the hike lasted 30 miles or 3000, life is never the same. The Walker is a different person.

People might confuse and enrage the post-walk Walker. Or, the post-walk Walker might want to hug every person in sight. Restlessness is the background level for the post-walk Walker. Every day, all day, there is a feeling of strained motionlessness, like the world might end unless you get out there and walk. And overcome with all the trappings of modern like—like TVs and car keys—the post-walk Walker often feels like he or she is forgetting something.

Worst of all, there are lingering questions about "what it all means". There is an overwhelming need to put some sort of meaning into the experience—"Well, I *did* it; now what does it *mean?*"

The secret is that there is no absolute answer to this question; thinking there is will drive a post-walk Walker mad unless or until he or she invents an answer.

* * *

Many post-walk Walkers gain a lot of weight after the trip. Conversely, some lose a lot of weight. Most people gain about 20 pounds in the couple of weeks following their Walk, I'd say.

Still, substantial weight gain or weight loss can sometimes be an indicator of depression. Walkers should keep an eye on their weight, and if they find themselves gaining or losing a lot of weight, they might want to spend time with a supportive group of people because it might be a symptom of depression.

* * *

M.W.C. 41.1: WHEN IT'S OVER, IT'S OVER, BUT *YOU* KEEP GOING.

Walkers should make sure to have a support network of people waiting for them when they finish their Walk. They should warn friends and family ahead of time that, after finishing, a Walker might be a little odd for a while. Best practice is to ask friends and family to be supportive, but also to be honest. Friends and family will ideally be honest to a Walker if his or her post-Walk behavior is strange or is causing discomfort to anyone else. When I got back from my Walk, I stayed with a couple of friends and the first thing I said (after thank you) was, "Listen, if I ever act weird or am doing something that makes you or anyone else uncomfortable, please tell me immediately and do not sugar coat it." That helped.

* * *

The Walker should take *time* when adjusting back to real life. The best advice I got after my walk was accidental. A county sheriff pulled over to see why I was sitting in the middle of nowhere in a car. After I told him that I was hiding from my family and friends, he told me to "take time; take time". It was the best advice I got.

* * *

Nothing will ever be the same, ever.

* * *

Some of the friends from before a Walk will no longer be a Walker's friends. Some will express jealousy, either openly or passive aggressively. Walkers might receive angry mail from people they don't even know. It's all a part of the process and Walkers should try not to stress about it.

* * *

Many friends will appear to have changed a great deal during a Walk. Walkers often come home to find that they now have nothing in common with some old friends. Relationships will change or they will end; Walkers should strive to do that peacefully and to have no hard feelings. Walkers feel like they are meeting all these people again for the first time.

They are right.

* * *

The moment you finish a cross-country hike (and in every moment that follows) you feel like you are meeting yourself for the first time.

You are.

GOOD LUCK

Appendix A

THE WALKOUT SYNDICATE

MODEL WALKING CODE (M.W.C.) 2013

WITH COMMENTS

PREAMBLE

[1]   It is apparent that freedom, dignity, adventure, and romance make it necessary, from time to time, to chuck it all and walk a very long way. Thus, various weaknesses and ills of modern culture make necessary the creation of a new, modern, secular pilgrimage (the "Walk"). Secular pilgrims ("Walkers") play a central role in preserving the principles of justice, freedom, progress, and discovery. Walkers must embody competence, integrity, and safety. The rules contained in this Code are precepts that Walkers, individually and collectively, should respect and honor in order to maintain public trust and to enhance the personal and collective benefits of the Walk.

[2]   Walkers should maintain dignity at all times and avoid both impropriety and the appearance of impropriety in their professional and personal lives. They should aspire at all times to conduct that ensures the greatest possible public confidence in their independence and competence.

[3]   The Model Walking Code establishes standards for the ethical and practical Walker. It is not intended as an exhaustive

guide for the conduct of Walkers who are governed in their general and personal conduct by general ethical and legal standards as well as by this Code. The Code is intended, however, to provide guidance and to assist Walkers in maintaining the highest standards of personal conduct.

SCOPE, INTERPRETATION, AND FURTHER REVIEW

[1]   The Model Walking Code consists of numbered rules and comments that follow and explain each Rule, where helpful or necessary.

[2]   The Rules state overarching principles of ethics, preparedness, and common sense. Where a Rule contains a permissive term, such as "may" or "should", the conduct being addressed is committed to the personal and professional discretion of the Walker.

[3]   The Comments that accompany the Rules serve two functions. First, they provide guidance regarding the purpose, meaning, and proper application of the Rules. Second, they contain explanatory material and, in some instances, provide examples of permitted or prohibited conduct.

[4]   The Rules are constantly subject to further review and may be changed by subsequent amendment.

The Model Walking Code
And Comments

RULE 1
Don't shit in your pants.

RULE 2
Don't be an asshole.

RULE 2.1
Don't hit anyone with a stout walking stick unless they swing first.
COMMENT
[1]   Rule 2.1 applies when conflict or disagreement cannot be resolved through peaceful means. "Unless they swing first" refers to any act of physical aggression, intimidation, or other act intended to place the walker in real or perceived danger. "Hit anyone with a stout walking stick" refers to any reasonable method of self-defense.
[2]   Walkers should aspire to pacifism and peaceful resolution of all conflict. Accordingly, each walker should comply with a strict rule of non-aggression. *See also* Rule 2.
[2]   Each Walker has the duty to defend him or her self, and the right to do so with any and all reasonable means.

RULE 3
Plan for water, always.
COMMENT
[1]   Rule 3 applies at all times. Water should be inventoried as often as possible. In instances where Rule 3 conflicts with Rule 11, a Walker should apply Rule 3.

[2]   Hiker Nate Damm advises that a hiker should "Top water bottles off constantly, at every chance."

RULE 3.1

You cannot carry all the water that you need in the desert.

COMMENT

[1]   Rule 3.1 is a specific application of Rule 3 and a general admonition to be aware of changing circumstances. Additionally, Rule 3.1 is intended to remind walkers that environmental realities are sometimes harsh and always changing.

[2]   For an example application of Rule 3.1, consider that water weighs roughly 8 pounds per gallon. It is the most burdensome limiting factor of any hike. In dry areas without access to either municipal water or surface water, hikers must carry large amounts of water. In the dry western portions of a cross-country hike, water needs almost certainly exceed carrying capacity unless the walker has car-support or a pushcart, or both.

RULE 3.2

Always carry with you a method of purifying water.

COMMENT

[1]   Rule 3.2 is a specific application of Rule 3 to all potential emergency situations. This rule recognizes that all planning, no matter how thoughtful and thorough, is subject to failure in emergency situations. *See also* Rule 20.

[2]   Regarding the appropriate method of water purification, water purification tablets are cheap and extremely lightweight and, accordingly, they should be carried at all times, even in conjunction with a water filter. Water filters of all kinds (including, but not limited to, UV filters and ceramic filters) are subject to clogging and/or mechanical failure. Water purification tablets, on the other hand, rarely fail and are a sound back-up plan.

RULE 3.3
The cleaner the water, the better the water.

COMMENT

[1]   Rule 3.3 works in conjunction with Rule 3 and Rule 3.2 to require vigilance in procuring clean, safe drinking water. In all instances where surface water must be harvested for drinking, all care should be taken to purify the water prior to ingestion. This will lessen the chances of sickness and infection. *See also* Rule 8.1.

[2]   Care should be taken to filter pathogens and contaminants from all surface water. Even in worst-case scenarios in which the Walker has no water purification tablets, no access to fuel for boiling, and no filtering device, the Walker should take all possible steps to clean water before drinking. A handkerchief over the opening in a water bottle will filter out large impurities and sediment, and time will allow sediment in the water to settle. Clear water left in direct sunlight for a few hours will often become marginally safer to drink.

RULE 4
Do not mix Spam and ramen noodles.

RULE 5
Know your trail, know yourself.

COMMENT

[1]   Rule 5 is immutable and applies in all instances, but is aspirational. In instances of conflict between Rule 5 and Rule 19, good luck. *But see* Rule 11.

RULE 6
It would be better if women ran the world; everyone would have a lot more fun.

RULE 6.1
The average woman is pretty stupid, but a lot smarter than the average man.

RULE 7
With every word you speak, decision you make, or action that you take, do everything in your power to limit, or to eradicate entirely, any unjustifiable harm that you would otherwise cause to another person, another living thing, or to the planet.

COMMENT

[1]   Rule 7 is a universal moral principle. It is the surest single rule by which to leave a moral, healthful, compassionate, and worthwhile life. It is immutable and applies in all instances.

[2]   Rule 7 begins from the principle that one should "do no harm". *See, e.g.*, the first principle of the medical profession, *'primum non nocere'* ('first, do no harm').

[3]   Rule 7 is derived in part from that maxim often termed the *"Golden Rule"*. Rule 7 encompasses both the *positive* form of The Golden Rule, *i.e.*, "do unto others as you would have them to unto you", and the *negative* form, *i.e.* "do not do unto others that which you would not have done to you".

[4]   Unlike the Golden Rule, Rule 7 is applicable in all instances. The Rule is made generally applicable by the limiting language of "to limit, or to eradicate entirely" and by the insertion of the word "unjustifiable".

[5]   In any instance of conflict between Rule 7 and Rule 11, it is best practice to apply Rule 7.

RULE 8
The Earth will kill you if you are not careful; it has no emotions.

COMMENT

[1]   Rule 8 reminds the Walker to be vigilant and humble and to always respect the power of nature. When on a Walk, a person willfully puts him or herself into a vulnerable position that can, at any moment, become gravely dangerous.

[2]   The second independent clause, "it has no emotions", is a rule against anthropomorphizing natural phenomena that might lead one to believe that the Earth has an interest in protecting a wayfaring Walker. It does not. This Rule is designed to prevent the Walker from romanticizing his or her relationship with the Earth.

RULE 8.1
There are some small things that you should worry about.
COMMENT

[1]   Rule 8.1 is directed specifically at very small organisms like viruses and bacteria. It is also a general rule, recognizing that high-stress, high-stakes situations sometimes call for a great deal of detail-oriented worrying.

[2]   For a specific application of Rule 8.1, consider the microorganisms causing Lyme disease and Rocky Mountain Spotted Fever. Ticks carry Lyme disease and Rocky Mountain Spotted Fever. Lyme Disease can produce symptoms for years and Rocky Mountain Spotted Fever has an untreated mortality rate around 35%. Insect repellent like DEET, although generally a harmful compound, is an effective tick repellent. On a cross-country hike, its value as tick repellent probably outweighs DEET's negatives.

[3]   Rule 8.1 also applies to the process of purifying water. *See* Rules 3.1 – 3.3.

RULE 8.2
Always check for widow-makers before pitching a tent.

RULE 8.3
We all end up buried, either by men or by the Earth.

COMMENT

[1]   Rule 8.3 is immutable. In instances of conflict between Rule 8.3 and other Rules, Rule 8.3 will apply.

[2]   This Rule is designed to remind the Walker that time does not stop and that we are all temporary. Accordingly, it is best practice to put every second of every life to the highest possible use.

RULE 8.4 [RESERVED]

COMMENT

[1]   If the proposed rule is adopted in future versions of the Model Walking Code, it should be read in conjunction with Rule 8.3.

RULE 9

The Sun will kill you if you are not careful; it has no emotions.

COMMENT

[1]   Rule 9 reminds the Walker to be vigilant and humble and to always respect the power of the Sun. When on a Walk, a person willfully puts him or herself into a vulnerable position that can become gravely dangerous.

[2]   Heat and prolonged exposure to direct sunlight can kill humans. The onset of heat exhaustion and hyperthermia is often quick. The best way to stay cool is to stay out of the direct sunlight, although shade is marginally less useful in humid conditions. An oversized golf umbrella is essential in the western states, where shade is difficult to find. *See also* Rule 14.

RULE 9.1

Get some Sun, but don't get burned.

COMMENT

[1]   When experiencing prolonged exposure to sunlight, the Walker should take steps to protect him or herself from sunburn.

Short-term exposure to sunlight, which triggers the tanning response, provides some prophylactic protection from subsequent sunburn. There is no substitute for sunscreen, though. *See* Rule 9.2.

RULE 9.2
Use sunscreen.

RULE 10
Speak less, say more.
COMMENT

[1]   Brevity is good.

RULE 10.1
98% of human communication is a waste of time.
COMMENT

[1]   Rule 10.1 is observational. It does not proscribe behavior. Rather, it recognizes a regrettable truth of the human condition and extols the Walker to monitor his or her own behavior accordingly.

[2]   Superfluous bloviating and loquaciousness are signs of weakness and low morals. Each is a symptom of society in decline. People talk to hear themselves talk and people write to fill up pages so that their publisher can charge more for information that one could probably find for free on Wikipedia or YouTube. The worst offenders are: 1) people on television, 2) authors/writers, and 3) lawyers.

[3]   For an example of this Rule in practice, *see generally* the Model Walking Code.

RULE 11
There are exceptions to every rule, including this one.
COMMENT

[1]   Rule 11 is immutable.

[2]   *Comment on conflict between Rule 11 and other Rules.* In instances of conflict between Rule 11 and Rule 7, best practice to apply Rule 7. In conflict between Rule 11 and Rule 3, best practice is to apply Rule 3. In conflict between Rule 11 and Rule 12, apply Rule 12.

RULE 12
Uncertainty is a law of the Universe.
COMMENT
[1]   In conflict between Rule 11 and Rule 12, apply Rule 12.

RULE 12.1
Don't predict; prepare.

RULE 12.2
You cannot plan for everything, but you cannot plan for *anything* unless you know your trail.

RULE 13
Life is a practice; walking is a practice.

RULE 14
When it's hot, keep cool; when it's cold, keep warm.

RULE 14.1
Evaporation cools down hot bodies.
COMMENT
[1]   Rule 14.1 is a specific application of science to Rule 14. Science is great. Evaporative cooling is a process by which the evaporation of water cools objects that are in contact with the water. This is generally the process by which sweat cools the human body and, given sufficient water, can be used to increase the cooling effect on the human body. A wet lightweight cloth on the head can help to cool the body in hot, dry conditions. If you have plenty of water, you

can soak a t-shirt or handkerchief in water and wrap that around a water bottle; the evaporation of the water from the kerchief will cool the water in the water bottle—a little.

RULE 14.2
Clothes should be versatile, not necessarily expensive.
COMMENT
[1]   The Walker should take all steps possible to save money when purchasing clothing. When assembling a wardrobe, the Walker should value versatility above brand name, hip factor, etc.

[2]   Clothes should be versatile enough to provide variable amounts of both warmth and protection from the Sun. A regular hiking shirt should be button down, not pullover, so that the wearer can better regulate heat loss by buttoning or unbuttoning the shirt, as appropriate. An unbuttoned shirt allows for greater ventilation and airflow close to the body, which can be substantially cooler than a pullover shirt. *See also* Rule 9.1, Rule 31.

RULE 14.3
Know your limitations.

RULE 14.4
[RESERVED]
Comment
[1]   Rule 14.4 is currently proposed, but not yet adopted. The proposed language would apply Rule 14.3 specifically to sleeping bags. It reads, "Know your limitations, but have a sleeping bag that is rated at least down to 20 degrees". It is unlikely that the proposed Rule will be adopted as currently drafted.

RULE 15

A human should know how to make fire, and how to respect it.

RULE 15.1
If you don't know how to build and maintain a fire, find someone to teach you.

RULE 15.2
Always carry two fire-starting tools.

RULE 15.3 [RESERVED]

RULE 16
Walk against traffic.
COMMENT
[1]   Rule 16 is both a specific rule for walking along highways and a general rule.

RULE 17
Be honest with yourself.

RULE 18
Be damned honest with yourself.

RULE 19
You are the biggest variable in your own life; do what you can to plan on that, if nothing else.
COMMENT
[1]   Rule 19 clarifies that Rule 5 is aspirational. It embodies the concept that all conditions and all people are capable of constant change.

RULE 19.1

Everyone should carry a small knife with them at all times.

RULE 19.2 [RESERVED].

RULE 20
Most essential planning is emergency preparedness; there will be emergencies.

RULE 21
Go west; start early.

RULE 22
Save money, always.

RULE 22.1
Don't buy expensive products when cheaper alternatives are available.
COMMENT
[1]   There are very cheap alternatives to many expensive items. For example, trash compactor bags are much thicker and more durable than trash bags, but are as effective as expensive dry bags at keeping clothes, sleeping bags, or food dry.

RULE 22.2
Expensive is not always better.

RULE 22.2.1
Don't pay for unnecessary technology.
COMMENT
[1]   Technology is great, but is often needlessly expensive. In hiking, especially, unnecessary technology makes otherwise

affordable objects cost-prohibitive. For example, external frame packs are about 1/3 the cost of internal frame packs.

[2]   Hiker Nate Damm commented, "I used a JanSport Carson external frame pack until I got a cart. Best pack ever and super cheap."

RULE 22.3
Some things are free.
COMMENT

[1]   Many items cost so little to produce that businesses offer them for free in hopes of attracting customers. For example, motels often offer travel combs for free. While travel combs are worthless as combs, they can be used to groom a dog and to remove ticks from the dog's fur. On a cross-country hike, it is important to groom any pets nightly to remove ticks. *See also* Rule 8.1, Rule 46.

RULE 22.4
Don't let anyone sell you things that you don't need.
COMMENT

[1]   Businesses rely on sales to make profit; often, it is in the business's interest to sell products and services that consumers neither need nor want. The process usually involves a lot of talking. *See also* Rule 10.1. Money should not be wasted on products that are unnecessary. For example, a "footprint" for a tent is not necessary; in the limited instances where a footprint might be helpful, a much cheaper tarp can be used instead. *See also* Rule 24, Rule 27.1. When using your tarp as a footprint, fold the extra material *under* the tarp itself so that the tarp is roughly the same size as the tent's floor.

RULE 22.5
Support local and independent businesses as often as possible.
COMMENT

[1]   Local and independent businesses often provide better service/products at cheaper prices. Widespread support of local and independent businesses supports a broader commercial system, safer from systemic shock. Independent motels, for example, are often quite affordable and are more likely to provide interaction with *interesting* people, as well as scary people. Many great stories are set in independent motels.

RULE 23
Cheaper is not always better.

RULE 23.1
Sometimes a dollar spent up front will save two dollars down the road.
COMMENT

[1]   This rule is a variation of the old saying, "A stitch in time saves nine." Where possible, future recurrent expenditures should be avoided by relatively larger up-front expenditures. For example, solid rubber tubes are more expensive that pneumatic tubes, but save both time and money on a cross-country hike because they do not have to be fixed or replaced. *But see* Rule 22.

RULE 24
Always have quick access to your tarp.

RULE 25 Simpler is better.

RULE 25.1
The simpler, the fewer things will go wrong.
COMMENT

[1]   Simple technology is usually better because fewer things will go wrong. For example, alcohol stoves are the best stove option for

90% of a cross-country hike and almost nothing can go wrong with or "break" an alcohol stove.

[2]   Note, also, that many nutritious, wonderful foods are so simple that they require no cooking. The Hiker should have some way of cooking, but about 85% of meals on a cross-country hike consist of food that doesn't need to be cooked.

RULE 26
Pack light and know how to use what you have.

RULE 27
Use what you have.

RULE 27.1
Find multiple uses for objects.
COMMENT

[1]   There are multiple uses for most items. Many items have alternative uses that are as valuable, or more valuable, than the intended use. For example, store your equipment on top of the picnic table at night and use the table to secure the tarp over your equipment. A water bottle can double as a duct tape storage unit if you wrap your water bottle with a couple layers of duct tap. Note that the duct tape will insulate the water bottle a little bit in addition to being a space-saving storage strategy for duct tape.

RULE 28
Pushing is easier than carrying.

RULE 29
Your body is a gift; treat it with respect.

RULE 29.1
Eat good food; don't eat garbage.

COMMENT

[1]   Do everything you can to avoid using gas stations as your primary source of food.

[2]   If you get cans of tuna, get the kind packed in oil and eat it all, including the oil.

[3]   Cross-country hikers need many calories and constantly strive to include good, healthful fats into the diet. Olive oil is a healthful, stable fat that travels well. Carry olive oil with you and add it liberally to everything.

RULE 29.2
Learn to do a full squat.
COMMENT

[1]   If you cannot do a full squat, do not attempt to walk across a continent. You will need to be able to squat, if you know what I'm saying.

RULE 29.3
Strengthen the weakest parts.
COMMENT

[1]   At the beginning of a long-distance hike, the three weak areas that will shorten days are feet, shoulders, and core, likely in that order; focus on strengthening those three areas and the walking will sort itself out on the trail.

RULE 29.3.1
Shoes weaken feet.
COMMENT

[1]   Rule 29.3.1 is a specific application of Rule 29, Rule 29.3, and Rule 22.2.1 to the feet. There was discussion as to whether this should qualify as a stand-alone rule.

[2]   In the months before a cross-county hike, spend as much time as you can barefoot; this will strengthen the muscles in your feet

and ankles and make you far less prone to injury. Spend several months strengthening your feet, no matter what kind of footwear you plan to wear.

RULE 30
Specialization is expensive.

RULE 30.1
Expensive purchases should have multiple uses.
COMMENT

[1]   Don't waste money and weight on a "footprint" for your tent; use a tarp if you need to.

[2]   If you get an internal frame pack, look for one with a detachable daypack on the top; you'll end up using the daypack quite a bit.

RULE 30.2
Reuse, repurpose; the dead and designers have no rights.
COMMENT

[1]   Many long distance hikers don't buy water bottles at all; instead, they re-use soda bottles or sports drink bottles; this is because long-distance hikes have the capacity to turn idiots into rational, thinking folks.

[2]   *See also* Rule 30.1, Comment 2.

RULE 31
Versatility is powerful.
COMMENT

[1]   Flossing is just as or more important than brushing; floss is lightweight and, in a pinch, can be used as twine or thread; floss every day if you can.

RULE 31.1
If you depend on something, it should be as versatile as possible.

Comment

[1]   A freestanding tent is a versatile tent.

RULE 32
Life is rhythmic.

RULE 33
It's better to rest than to die.

RULE 33.1
Time lost to injury prevention is time not lost.

Comment

[1]   Stop the second you feel a hot spot or think you might be getting a blister; immediately treat the blister and take steps to prevent aggravating the spot.

RULE 34
Failure is always an option.

RULE 35
If you have it, know how to use it; if you don't know how to use it, don't have it.

RULE 35.1
Don't rely on equipment until you've learned to use it.

Comment

[1]   No matter what kind of pack you get, make sure to wear it fully loaded on a few long hikes before you head out for your big long hike to make sure it fits.

RULE 36
Walking is a practice.

RULE 36.1 [RESERVED]

RULE 37
Some people are crazy; try to stay away from crazy people.

RULE 37.1
Sometimes it is difficult to distinguish the crazy ones from the sane ones.
COMMENT

[1]	Hiker Nate Damm comments, "More than one car in the driveway is typically a good sign; two insane people living together is much less likely than one crazy person living alone."

RULE 38
When you need to hide, be hidden.
COMMENT

[1]	For specific application of Rule 38, consider tents and tarps. Walkers should consider getting tents and tarps that are muted colors, often either brown or green, so that they might better remain hidden while stealth camping.

RULE 38.1
Technology and comfort both sometimes draw attention.
COMMENT

[1]	In stealth camping there is NO cooking, NO open flame, NO music, NO flashlight, and NO smart phone; don't use any technology that emits light or sound.

RULE 38.2
Don't hide in dangerous places.

RULE 39
When you need to be visible, be visible.

RULE 39.1
Don't rely on other people to see you when you need to be seen.
COMMENT
[1]   Store your yellow rain jacket on the outside of your pack or cart to increase your visibility.

RULE 40
Don't predict, prepare.

RULE 41
You can't do it alone.

RULE 41.1
When it's over, it's over, but you keep going.
COMMENT
[1]   A support network of friends and family is priceless; make sure to have one in place before you finish a long walk.

RULE 41.2 Try to make a good impression.
COMMENT
[1]   Rule 41.2 is the application of Rule 50 to first impressions with humans.
[2]   Carry a travel-sized bottle of mouthwash and a high-powered deodorant just in case you have to make a "good impression".

[3]   Develop an "elevator pitch"; for yard camping, make it short, friendly, and exciting; smile a lot, but not too much.

RULE 41.3
Half the value of any good experience is in sharing it with others.
COMMENT
[1]   Great pictures make your memories accessible to friends and family; a nice camera is neither essential nor lightweight, but it can make your trip accessible to people you love. The people you love want to see mountains, and they also want to see you; make sure to get pictures of yourself during your trip.

RULE 42
You depend on people, whether you admit it or not; people depend on you, whether they admit it or not.

RULE 42.1
Your actions and inactions affect other people.
COMMENT
[1]   Rule 42.1 works in conjunction with Rule 42 to embody the principle that all humans (and all living creatures) are connected and interdependent.
[2]   Rule 42.1 should be applied in all instances. For example, when in bear country, 1) always use a bear bag or bear canister, 2) always clean up after yourself, and 3) never feed the bears. Otherwise, bears may become accustomed to eating human refuse, will lose their fear of humans, and will become "problem bears".

RULE 42.2 [RESERVED]

RULE 43

If someone invites you to sleep on their yard or in their house, eat whatever they offer you.

RULE 44
Information is worth its weight in gold.

RULE 44.1
Scout out the future.

COMMENT

[1]   Rule 44.1 applies Rule 44 to future conditions. When possible, future conditions should be scouted ahead of time in order to acquire useful information. *See also* Rule 12.2. *But see* Rule 12.

[2]   Use Google Maps terrain feature to estimate the elevation changes you will have to overcome in the mountains. Use the Google Maps satellite feature to scout potential stealth camping spots and potential shade spots ahead of time.

RULE 45
Be humble.

RULE 46
Cleanliness.

RULE 46.1
Brush your teeth every day; flossing is more important.

RULE 46.2
If you stay in a motel or a campground with a sink, wash your clothes in the sink before you go to sleep and hang them up with plenty of time for them to dry before you want to leave in the morning.

RULE 47
Slow, careful work is fast work.

RULE 47.1
Preparation makes a slow job faster.
COMMENT
[1]   Rule 47.1 applies specifically to any task that will likely be repeated. For example, the hikers should save time by affixing lengths of rope or twin to the corners of a tarp; three lengths can be short, but one should be pretty long. *See also* Rule 47, Rule 47.2.

RULE 47.2
Organization makes a slow job faster.
COMMENT
[1]   Designate a medium-sized stuff sack as your "tent sack" and fill it with all of the items that you need to have with you in the tent at night; learn to recognize this particular sack by look *and* by texture.

RULE 48
Stay dry when it counts.

RULE 48.1
Don't sleep wet.
COMMENT
[1]   Sleeping bags should always be stored in a waterproof container, like a trash compactor bag.

RULE 49
Don't be so scared all the time.

RULE 49.1

A (wo)man ain't no (wo)man if (s)he can't walk across a continent without a gun.

RULE 49.2
If you're afraid to walk across the country without a gun, stay at home.

RULE 50
Appearances shouldn't matter; they do.

RULE 50.1
If you look dirty, people think you're dirty.

COMMENT

[1] Rule 50.1 is an application of Rule 50 to physical appearances. People in vulnerable situations, like a cross-country hike, should take steps to monitor and maintain a clean appearance. *See* Rule 50.

[2] Do not wear white or light colored pants.

RULE 50.2
If you look dangerous, don't be surprised when people are afraid of you.

RULE 51
It is almost certainly not the end of the world; be cool.

RULE 51.1
Don't take yourself so seriously.

RULE 51.2
Don't sweat the big things, either.

COMMENT

[1]   Rule 51.2 is an extension of Rule 51 and is designed to make Rule 51 applicable in all instances.

[2]   Regarding application of Rule 51 to stealth camping, Nate Damm comments, "It doesn't make sense to get upset, frustrated, or scared when you can't find a place to sleep. When it gets dark, you can hide pretty much anywhere there is a shadow, and there are plenty to choose from. Worst-case scenario, you have to get up really early. That's no big deal. There is ALWAYS some place to sleep."

RULE 52
Fabric is important.

COMMENT

[1]   Rule 52 is designed to remind people of the importance of fabric material and of using the right material for the right purpose. Rule 52 also refers to the general prohibition against cotton for high exertion activities, such as hiking. In general, cotton is for sleeping, lounging, and very little else. *See also* Rule 52.1, Rule 52.2.

RULE 52.1
No cotton.

RULE 52.2
No cotton socks.

RULE 53
Go an extra mile when it matters.

COMMENT

[1]   Generally speaking, the easiest way to accomplish a given task is the best way to accomplish a given task. However, in higher stakes matters, it is sometimes best practice to take extra steps to protect yourself, your plan, or your equipment. This is especially true when the extra measures are low or no cost. For example, it is not necessary to stake out or guy out a freestanding tent, but this should

still be done in all instances where staking and guying are possible. *See also* Rule 54.

RULE 53.1 [RESERVED]

RULE 54
If it's that important, have a back up.
COMMENT

[1] Redundancy is the quality of having one or more back-ups in place to protect against failure of a primary device or plan. When in high-stress, high-stakes situations, such as a cross-country hike, redundant measures should be in place to protect against failure of important devices and plans. For example, it is best practice to keep at least one extra cell phone battery with you and charged at all times.

RULE 54.1 [RESERVED].

RULE 55
Everyone should know how to tie five good knots.

RULE 56
Don't count on anyone 100%.

RULE 56.1
[RESERVED]

RULE 57
Don't steal.

RULE 57.1
Some things can be used for free.
COMMENT

[1]   There is a general prohibition against stealing. However, some things can be used for free. In some instances, free use of a privately owned resource is either implied or not specifically outlawed. In those instances, it is sometimes morally accepted for a person to rely on implied permission to temporarily use very small amounts of that resource. *But see* Rule 57.

[2]   There are WiFi access points all across the United States at motels, parks, homes, and even gas stations in the middle of nowhere. Some are password protected and some are not. In most cases, if there is no password protecting the network, one might understand that there is implied permission for free use.

[3]   There are power outlets all over the place—in municipal parks, outside gas stations, behind grocery stores; using these may not be "legal", but it is "possible".

[4]   *See* Rule 7.

FROM THE AUTHOR AND CONTRIBUTORS

I hope you enjoyed this book.

If you're thinking about a long-distance hike, take the trip seriously. You can laugh about it, but respect it.

Experiences like this change the way a person interacts with the world.

Usually for the better.

You will own all of the memories from the trip.

Memories will come back to you when you least expect them.

You will have done something that few *could* do and that even fewer *have* done.

It will be very difficult to intimidate you and very difficult to scare you.

It might help you to be happy.

I want you to be happy.

THIS PAGE IS BLANK. MAYBE YOU SHOULD WRITE ON IT.

This guy did it:

He is Nate Damm. He crossed in 2011.

He started at Cape Henlopen, Delaware, in February of 2011 and finished at Ocean Beach in San Francisco in October of 2011.

He walked "3200 miles or so, not completely sure."

You can read more about Damm and his walk at www.natedamm.com.

THIS PAGE IS BLANK. MAYBE YOU SHOULD WRITE ON IT.

This lovely couple did it, too:

They are Kait Whistler Seyal and John Seyal. They crossed America in 2012.

They started in Lewes, Delaware and finished in Long Beach, California.

You can read more about Team Seyal and their walk at www.dogblogusa.com.

THIS PAGE IS BLANK. MAYBE YOU SHOULD WRITE ON IT.

And this fellow did it:

Tyler Coulson walked across the United States in 2011.

He started from Rehoboth Beach, Delaware, in March of 2011 and ended in Ocean Beach, San Diego, CA, in November of 2011.

You can read more about his walk in his 2012 book, BY MEN OR BY THE EARTH. You can find it at www.tylercoulson.com or on Amazon.

WE HAVE A BEAUTIFUL WORLD TO WALK AROUND IN, FOR NOW. GET OUT IN IT.

THIS PAGE IS BLANK. MAYBE YOU SHOULD WRITE ON IT.

6400256R10150

Printed in Germany
by Amazon Distribution
GmbH, Leipzig